Foresight 2010

Disclaimer

This publication and all or any of its contents are provided for information use only. Exclusive Analysis Ltd accepts no responsibility or liability for any use that may be made of all or any of the contents or any acts or omissions reliant in whole or in part thereon.

Published by
Exclusive Analysis Ltd, 68 Lombard Street, London, EC3V 9LJ, UK
Email: info@exclusive-analysis.com
Tel: +44 (0) 20 7868 1629
Web: www.exclusive-analysis.com

ISBN: 978-0-9561367-1-8

Intelligence cut-off date
20 October 2009

Our articles contain forward-looking statements. We recommend that you visit the relevant country pages on our Country Risk Evaluation and Assessment Model (CREAM) for an updated view.

Printed and bound by Europa (Printing Group), London

Cover images (from L to R, Front cover to Back)
• Green Point Stadium, Cape Town, Rotsee2 (November 2008), *Wikimedia commons, licensed under the Creative Commons Attribution ShareAlike 3.0 License*
• President of Petrobras, Sergio Gabrielli (L) and president Lula da Silva (R) during a visit to the P-34 offshore platform (2008), *ABr / Ricardo Stuckert*
• Company A, 2nd Battalion, 22nd Infantry Regiment, 10th Mountain Division. U.S. Army, *photo by Staff Sgt. Kyle Davis, Wikipedia commons. This work is in the public domain in the United States because it is a work of the United States Federal Government under the terms of Title 17, Chapter 1, Section 105 of the US Code.*
• Chinese President Hu Jintao visiting Kenya, Fredrick Onyango (2006), *Wikimedia commons, licensed under the Creative Commons Attribution ShareAlike 3.0 License*
• Panoramic view of containers in a harbour, © *iStockphoto.com/diego cervo (Extended License)*
• Prime Minister of Zimbabwe Morgan Tsvangirai with portrait of Zimbabwe President Robert Mugabe (2007). *Source: Shepherd Tozvireva*

Contributors

Editors

Simon Sole, Elizabeth Kelleher, Kirsten Parker, Michael Simms, Richard Bond, John Cochrane, Alex Poole-Warren, David Hunt, Rachel Shoemaker, Zaineb al-Assam, Rafael Gomes

Contributors

OB Sisay, Thoko Kaime, John Raines, Carlos Caicedo, Paul McGrath, Rachel Shoemaker, Arvind Ramakrishnan, Teymur Huseynov, Joanna Gorska, Zaineb al-Assam, Faysal Itani, Pepe Egger, Anna Murison, Rafael Gomes, Nathalie Wlodarczyk, Richard Bond, David Hunt, John Cochrane, Jennifer Booth, Andy Gardner, Cathy Wilford, Phuchong Suriwong, Kirsten Parker, Simon Sole, Michael Simms, Elizabeth Kelleher, Alex Poole-Warren, Phil Skinner, Georgie Elston, Lee Foster, Ed Lowes, Anna Mathewson, Paul Clayton, R. Alexander Hamilton, Julia Hulme, Leonid Peisakhin, Alisa Lockwood, Prashant Sawant, Hamir Sahni, Leon Ittiachen, Andy Webb-Vidal, Guillermo Parra-Bernal, Winston Moore, Daniel Collyns, Eduardo Crawley, Stephan Küffner, Patrick Timmis, Robert Besseling, Matthew Johnson, Francois Toerien, Jarret Brachman, Chris Boucek, Peter Cole, Omar Ashour

Administrative and Operational Support

Sangita Sanghrajka, Jennifer Booth, Sarah Higson, Jacquie Sole

Production and Design

Hana Tanimura, Alex Poole-Warren, Phil Skinner

Table of contents

Eurasia and Western Europe

Latin America

Middle East and Northern Africa

Introduction

Turning Insight Into Foresight

I. Foreword

Simon Sole, MPhil (Cantab), BSc, FRGS
CEO, Exclusive Analysis Ltd

I do hope this yearbook challenges. We held a workshop with external guests called 'Confronting Uncertainty' in June to stimulate ideas for our yearbook, and we plan to repeat this each year. This year's articles on The Evolution of Economic Warfare and Forecasting the Unprecedented – What is Forward-Looking Data? aim to spark new areas of thought for the reader. Other articles, such as those on Iran, Pakistan and Venezuela, examine how complex political situations will evolve in 2010 and what they will mean for political and violent risk environments. As ever, the Global Risk Outlook gives a snapshot of what we expect to happen in many countries in 2010.

I was surprised to discover how little consensus there is, even amongst risk professionals, about what risk actually is and what the word means. All agree that it is risky to climb a cliff without a rope. Few think it is risky to jump off a cliff to a certain death, despite that being the worst thing that could happen when climbing without a rope. The outcome was known. Most think it risky for a female to run in shorts in Afghanistan because, like ropeless climbing, something dangerous is very likely to happen, but you don't know quite what! It is not considered risky to buy a lottery ticket since the uncertainty is on the upside, despite the fact that the biggest risk to most corporations is failure to identify an opportunity before a competitor takes advantage of it. So it seems the word 'risk' emphasises downside uncertainty, but the elements of it are much broader. Moving beyond a static idea of risk, we focus on understanding individual clients' risk appetites, on finding differences between the perception and reality of risk and, most importantly, on identifying opportunities.

We try to think clearly about risk and streamline our services to clients in tight, simple and unambiguous forecasts (see The Language of Risk). Too much information is not just overwhelming for clients, it's toxic. Successful organisations identify key information faster and interpret it more accurately than their competitors. We constantly scan the horizon to pick out what's important and stream it to those for whom it's most relevant.

We also numerate risk in a bid to help those who must price it, and assist those allocating resources to mitigate physical risk (see Indexing Human Safety). And of course our global network of sources and analysts works hard to highlight improving risk environments to our clients. This can lead to them reallocating financial or physical assets between territories, and in some cases new market entry.

Looking into 2010, the contest of ideas has yet to take shape. The major economic powers disagree on several key policy issues, including how to sequence the end of fiscal stimulus, redress trade and monetary imbalances and reform financial sector remuneration. But the tactical breadth of these debates contrasts with the more strategic agendas of the last half century (e.g. capitalism vs. socialism or Keynesianism vs. a neo-liberal 'Washington Consensus'). With many saying that the so-called Washington Consensus has died, the scarcity of 'big think' in the public and private sectors is notable.

Before I sign off, I'd like to thank our clients for their continued trust and support and I hope to see lots of you in 2010. Many of you drop in to our daily Global Intelligence Briefings from time to time. If you haven't done this but would like to (clients or non-clients), please just let us know. And if something in this yearbook surprises you, or if you find an article especially interesting, please get in touch. Many have done this over the years and it's a great way to start a dialogue. Welcome to Foresight 2010.

II. About Exclusive Analysis

As a specialist intelligence company, our core expertise is gathering extensive historical and forward-looking data that enables us to spot trends ahead of others. We feed these inputs into a structured analytical process and employ a suite of tools, including location intelligence inputs, modelling techniques and scenario analysis to forecast accurately. The deliverables are tailored to clients to help them identify risk and opportunities globally and to maximise their strategic planning efforts.

Our People

We work with data, models and systems, but, in the end, forecasting is a product of informed human judgment. Exclusive Analysis is passionate about creating the right culture to produce objective and accurate analysis. Our vision is to systematise the qualitative and subjective art of political risk analysis to deliver numerated, accurate forecasts on which clients can act with confidence. We recruit from all over the world to bring together people with a deep understanding of different regions, multilingual capabilities and technical expertise.

One of the challenges (and pleasures) of our work is integrating knowledge to produce a holistic view. This might mean thinking about Iran from a Russian/Iraqi/US/European and, of course, Iranian perspective. This way we are much more likely to determine the correct pathway of future events. Or it might mean integrating economics with cultural issues, demographic and legal analysis to forecast future business environments.

Our Clients

Our clients work in many different roles in a variety of sectors including financial services, natural resources, shipping, aviation, cargo, government and non-governmental organisations and (re)insurance. Delivery against their unique requirements is key to our offering. For example, for a corporate security manager in an energy company we provide forecasts to build business continuity plans. For an insurance underwriter, we deliver intelligence to improve risk selection or support knowledge-based pricing. For a government agency, we provide robust decision-support tools that help evaluate policy options.

We work hard to know our clients well, to establish high levels of trust and to interact frequently, and often informally, with them. We try to anticipate how they will use our analysis, and the internal questions they are likely to face, to ensure that our output is absolutely tailored to that client.

Teamwork:	We are committed to a common goal – producing the best forecasts. We want to attract and retain the best people from around the world. We emphasise team-building, and we train, challenge and mutually respect each other.
Objectivity:	We are independent forecasters, not advocates, and we do not use judgmental or biased language. We challenge assumptions.
Commercial Relevance:	We forecast commercial risks and opportunities. Our work is customised for clients and is country, sector, asset, company or deal specific.
Client-Facing:	We work hard to think from the client's perspective. How will they use our reports?
Trust:	'We tell you what we know; we tell you what we don't know; we tell you what we think; we never confuse the three.'
Innovation:	We seek new sources and unique information, and we approach questions from new angles. We are professionalising analysis by constantly developing our models and methodologies.
Precision:	We provide detailed forecasts and use specific language. We communicate both quantitatively and qualitatively.

Key Deliverables

Country Risk Evaluation and Assessment Model (CREAM) is our flagship online risk model that forecasts political risk, civil unrest, terrorism and war risk in every country, across asset type and location. It includes over 6,000 forecasts and assessments, 350,000+ fully searchable risk-relevant historical data points, risk indices and risk mapping tools. The CREAM Service includes a proactive delivery of customised streamed intelligence to clients.

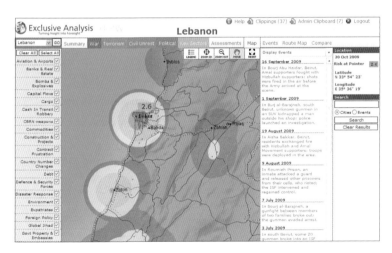

Tailored Forecasts and Counter-party Analysis assesses specific risks and opportunities to a country, sector, local partner, company, asset, investment or portfolio based on the client's specific interests and exposures.

Strategic Services and Risk Management are part of a highly interactive consulting relationship with clients. Decision-support tools we deliver include:

Strategic Trends Forecasting and Futures Analysis, Critical Scenario Selection and Stress-Testing Models, Probable Maximum Loss/Value at Risk Analysis, Customised Risk and Opportunity Indices and Risk Discounted Cash-Flow Modelling.

Watch Lists and Indices can be produced to clients' specification in order to inform one-off decision processes or to maintain a real-time, quantified assessment of relative risks.

Analyst Contact and Opportunity Briefings allow clients to access the analytical team in the Global Intelligence Centre directly.

Intelligence, Analysis and Methodology Training is available to clients on analysis and forecasting methodology or on content areas (countries, sectors or technical issues).

TerrorRisk is a location mapping layer that assesses the relative terrorism risk at over 4,700 global points of interest in 40 cities within 19 countries. The tool can be integrated into existing geospatial systems and platforms.

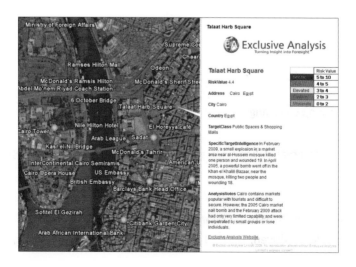

III. The Language of Risk

This article examines how the language used to assess and analyse is in fact as important as the forecast itself. Everyday phrases like 'al-Qaeda', 'corruption' and 'international community' are loaded; we identify such language and seek to be more rigorous and precise. Risk management and risk assessment decisions, be they tactical pricing decisions or strategic institutional decisions, rely upon the interpretation of information. In a world in which information bombards us from every angle, clear and concise language is essential for specific, actionable forecasts.

Successful organisations identify key information faster and interpret it more accurately than their competitors. Relevance and brevity are therefore crucial. As Blaise Pascal said, and Mark Twain paraphrased, 'I am sorry for the length of my letter, but I hadn't time to write a short one.'

Casual use of language undermines the value of risk assessments. Some common examples of imprecise use of language are highlighted below.

Biased or Loaded Language

'Hopefully', 'unfortunately', 'necessary', 'worrying', 'troubling' and other judgmental words – Risk analysis involves objective forecasting, not advocacy; subjective language suggests bias or an agenda.

'Rational', 'pragmatic', 'ideological', 'radical', 'populist' – These words are used casually, but to call a leader or a group 'rational' or 'irrational' is to make a value judgment about how that actor has defined their own strategic interests. 'Pragmatic' is much the same; often used to imply that an actor is not ideologically driven, it avoids analysis of the full range of strategic interests and neatly ignores that all actors are ideologically driven, but just by different ideologies! By 'populist', do we mean advocating increased spending on social services, supporting nationalisation, referring to emotive ideological issues to gather support or spending money in key constituencies? As ever, precision adds value in a way that flippant labels do not.

'For political reasons' – This conveys bias or agenda, as if a government acting for political reasons was wrong or unusual.

'Government interference' (e.g. in commercial operations) – Government actors will always participate in the commercial space, setting policies, developing and interpreting regulation and, indeed, even sometimes bailing out companies. The word 'interference' in this context is loaded.

'Rocked', 'stormed' – These words are visceral and dramatic (as in 'a bomb rocked the hotel', 'police stormed the building'). This type of language is more suited to a headline than to political analysis.

'Regime' – It is important to use this word consistently rather than refer to certain governments as 'regimes' and others as 'administrations' or 'governments'. We can use all of these words to describe the organised leadership of a country, so long as we consistently use them interchangeably (e.g. not always calling the leadership in country X a 'regime' and in country Y a 'government'). If we are seeking to communicate that a government is not popularly elected or that there are certain ways it contains dissent (banning protests, arresting opposition supporters, etc.) it is better to say so clearly than to use casual shorthand. We use the phrase 'regime stability' to describe the probability that the current leadership will remain in power over a defined period of time. This phrase applies equally to the leadership in Iran, the US, Zimbabwe and France.

Imprecise Language

'Hallmarks' (as in 'the attack had all the hallmarks of al-Qaeda') – It is far more useful to provide specific details on the characteristics of an attack or a group's tactics, in particular the target, location, timing and mode and size of an attack.

'Links', 'ties', 'connections' – Almost anything can be 'linked'. What is the nature or extent of a relationship? Is there simply a common ideology or common enemy between the two parties? Is there an exchange of funding, personnel, training or other resources?

'Tensions' (as in 'tensions will rise on the border') – What are the tensions and how will they impact on business risk? Is there a specific demarcation dispute that will lead to a pitched battle between troops or a risk of licence cancellation for businesses in disputed areas? Do we mean that a trade dispute between two countries will lead to new regulations and cargo disruption? Is communal violence between ethnic groups in a certain town more likely? On what scale and in what time frame? Who and what will be affected?

'Charismatic' – A leader may indeed have a strong following or be widely acknowledged as a compelling speaker, but it is helpful to be more detailed about to whom exactly the leader's style or views appeal to and to what end. Likewise, analysts should assess the content, medium and tone of communication used.

'Instability' or 'unstable' – Instead of referring to 'political instability' it is better to describe the fact that a coalition government is likely to fracture, that snap elections are likely to be called, that a military coup is imminent or that a popular movement calling for a dramatic change of leadership is emerging. Further, it is crucial to describe the implications for policies, disputes and key risks and opportunities.

'Clashes' – 'Clashes' can take many forms: fighting between police and protesters, policy disputes between rival parties in a parliamentary debate, small arms fire between militias, pitched battles between standing armies, etc. The difference between these is central to specific judgments and must be made clear.

'Reportedly', 'is expected to', 'analysts say' – According to whom? It is useful to be clear about who exactly is reporting, expecting or saying something.

'Fundamentalist' – Fundamentalism is not the same as extremism or militancy, and these words must not be used interchangeably.

'FARC', 'al-Qaeda', 'Taliban', etc. – Not many jihadis can be credibly called al-Qaeda, as 'al-Qaeda' implies a structure and level of hierarchy that we assess is overstated. Likewise, not all violence in Colombia and Afghanistan can be attributed to the FARC or the Taliban, respectively. We are careful in attributing attacks to a certain actor, especially where it is not very clear who was responsible. Casual attribution can confuse the risk picture in important ways.

'Massive' and 'huge' – These lack precision and are often driven by emotion, so their use should be sparing.

'Short, medium and long term' – 'Long' might refer to China's 20-year evolution into a market economy. In the Iraq War, however, it means three months. Time periods must be quantified.

Jargon and Buzzwords

'Globalisation' – It is much more useful to talk about particular dynamics or consequences than to use an abstract reference. For instance, referencing a specific trade dispute, migration pattern or specific forecasts in an emerging market adds much more value. This word is also often used in a loaded, normative context.

'Failed state' – This term is often used to describe a state in which the central government does not have full territorial control, and/or where there have been persistent economic difficulties (very high unemployment, high debt, etc.), non-participation in international bodies, several non-functioning institutions (for instance, non-independence of courts, dissolution of parliament or non-delivery of health services) or extensive cooperation between officials and criminal organisations. This term may be useful for policymakers or advocates to generate interest, but for analysts, definition of the exact conditions adds far more value.

'Crisis' – What is the benchmark for something being a crisis? Is there a less emotive, more descriptive way of communicating the issue?

'Legitimacy' – Who is to judge legitimacy and what is the measure? There can be opposition to a fairly and popularly elected government from internal or external detractors. A government may have passed an unpopular policy or lost points in opinion polls. But if it is not impeachable or if there is not a no-confidence vote, who is to determine the threshold for a government being 'illegitimate'? Also, it does not follow that 'legitimacy' or a lack thereof leads to one outcome or another. It is more useful to say that an opposition movement will almost certainly unseat a government in coming elections, or that a military coup is likely in the coming six months or that the government has lost bargaining power with another key international player to some specific end.

'Governance' and 'corruption' – These terms are often used as shorthand where a more precise term would be available. 'Good governance' is a very subjective term, and it is too easy to talk loosely about 'governance problems' in developing countries when in fact there are issues of institutional and political reform in the West that are similarly analysable. 'Corruption' is also problematic. These words are a red flag signalling that an analyst should elaborate. By 'corruption' do we mean bid fixing, bribery or political favouritism? There is a risk of falling prey to double standards. It is easy to miss corporate tax fraud or nepotism, which occur in highly developed markets as well emerging markets. By saying exactly what we mean, we avoid generalisations about 'corruption in Africa', for example, and can talk more usefully about corruption in a more concrete way.

'International community' – The 'international community' is unhelpful as an analytical concept. In the first place, there is disagreement about what it means (shared values, a shared identity or a shared forum?). Indeed, there is not one unitary community, but rather a collection of interests that are more often than not competing. The 'international community' does not have a view of nuclear enrichment in Iran; rather, there are competing views held by China, the US, the EU, Russia, etc. It is of greater value to analyse the interests of these different actors and to forecast their likely actions.

The Language of Probability

'Will remain' – Concluding that something has been, is and will continue to be an issue is of use, but it is generally of greater interest to elucidate a new trend or new development that adds nuance to our understanding or makes current assumptions problematic.

'There are great uncertainties' – This is precisely why risk analysis is required. Borrowing a reader's watch to tell him the time is not what he has a right to expect.

'Should', 'may' or 'could' – These convey only expectation or unqualified potential. Risk analysis must ascribe a probability.

'Cannot be ruled out', 'too early to tell', 'remains to be seen' – Nothing can be ruled out, especially in high-risk operating environments. If there is a small chance of a certain scenario coming to fruition, highlighting the potential impact(s), while noting the probability or otherwise, adds value. Simply refusing to 'rule out' a scenario amounts to an analyst hedging his or her bets at the expense of a decisive, well-qualified forecast.

'High', 'moderate', 'low' – Labels are very useful, for instance in communicating relative risk in indices. In qualitative analysis, it is useful for analysts to describe the detail behind those labels. How large and frequent will bomb attacks be? How many companies will be nationalised and in which sectors?

'Increasing', 'rising', 'decreasing' – We can use historical data to demonstrate a trend. We can also use forward-looking data to make a projection or a forecast. But it is important not to conflate the two exercises. For example, it would not be rigorous to conclude that 'there was a kidnapping of an aid worker in country X, therefore the risk of aid workers being kidnapped in country X is increasing'.

It is clear that when an analyst writes that something is 'likely', on balance they have judged it will happen, but there is almost always scope to add far more precision to a forecast.

First, it is important to provide detail around exactly *what* is likely. To say that 'mining strikes are likely' is less actionable than to say 'at least 70% of copper miners working at mines x, y and z are likely to go on strike in July, with those mines almost certain to be operating at very limited capacity or not at all for at least seven days'. Of course, the more specific the forecast, the less likely it is to come exactly true, but we judge that it is better to be precise than never to be wrong because we have never actually made a judgment of any substance. To express probability without detail is of limited use.

Second, there are many gradients of probability. Codifying and quantifying probability can help the reader. Rather than a binary 'likely'/'unlikely' model, the analyst can assign a percentage to the probability. The analyst can also use a range of phrases along the spectrum of probability, from 'near certain' on one end of the spectrum to 'likely' and 'distinct possibility' through to 'highly improbable' at the other end. For less actionable phrases like 'distinct possibility' we would always challenge the analyst to go further in identifying what the triggers or indicators for that outcome would be.

Finally, even in circumstances where the analyst is not able to make a forecast because, for example, a key piece of information is not available, it is still possible to go further with scenario analysis. Separately assessing the probability of, indicators for and outcomes of different developments pathways can add great value by indicating what would make a certain outcome more probable (and how much more probable). Scenario analysis also allows for the relative probability of different scenarios to be assessed (e.g. even if the absolute probability of a scenario is difficult to ascertain it is often possible to determine its relative likelihood).

1. Global

Turning Insight Into Foresight

1. The Global Risk Outlook for 2010

The context of 2010 is one of relief for governments and surviving financial institutions that there has not been the apocalyptic global financial collapse that seemed a distinct possibility in early 2009. The banking system remains intact even if in the West it responds sluggishly to government requests to lend or cap bonuses. Global stock markets and commodities have rebounded strongly since March 2009, and default risk priced into the debt of weaker borrowers has fallen dramatically.

The restored financial system is still too close to the one that broke down though. The injection of unprecedented levels of liquidity has meant that much of the faltering machinery of capitalism has yet to be questioned, much less reformed. Western accounting practices, despite the expense, have a poor track record of forecasting failure, particularly when companies are in distress. The basis for asset valuation, particularly of property and complex derivative products, is not transparent or reliable. Rating agencies still look backwards more than forwards. The revolution in financial regulation that many expected has not materialised. Regulators have focused on enforcing old rules and tightening reserve requirements.

Improved information is now in the hands of government planners, which may seduce them, once again, to think they can allocate capital better than the market. Centrally controlled economies can indeed respond more decisively to shocks; China's control of its banks being a case in point. However, the markets almost certainly remain the most efficient mechanism for allocating capital. In short, we do not think the age of capitalism has passed, but its operating machinery probably needs much more reform.

The obvious hard political choices are still not yet fully on the agenda. Discussion of deficit reduction has not really addressed the political and cultural costs of welfare reduction. The need for popular support is undermined by low trust in politicians (especially in the UK, with falling electoral participation and cynicism following the MPs' expenses scandal). How will economies that have relied so heavily on consumer debt driven growth move forwards, as consumers reverse previous excesses and pay down their debts? Will economic growth be anaemic in the US and UK for another decade as governments tighten fiscal policies to reduce budget deficits? And will monetary policies remain super-loose for years in an environment of protracted fiscal tightening?

Power has certainly ebbed away from Western states but it has yet to find a new base for political expression. It is though clear that much of the investment capital for relatively riskier, growth-inducing activities (e.g. infrastructure development) is predominantly in non-Western hands. The G8 is now the G20.

Western military powers and political ideas are likewise globally less welcome than they were and have to be delivered as if between peers and not imposed. The UK did not end the effortless condescension we referred to in Foresight 2009 quite soon enough and was as good as kicked out of Iraq. The UK assumed it would remain welcome in Iraq for largely historical reasons and, in fact, Prime Minister al-Maliki saw little further utility in a British presence.

What happens in Afghanistan in 2010 will be the key indicator of whether President Obama has managed to change the trajectory of US global power. No matter which precise strategy is adopted, there is consensus that change is needed, with President Obama signalling a clear preference for a period of intensive effort leading to a drawdown in about two years, before he starts campaigning for a second term. No matter how it is resourced, which at the time of writing is being debated, the strategy hinges on effective training of an Afghan Army and police to take over most of the duties of the International Security Assistance Force (ISAF). It also relies on applying styles and techniques that were used to co-opt the Sunni tribes in Iraq in order to encourage those now fighting the ISAF to renounce the Taliban and align themselves with the Karzai government.

It is unclear why training the Afghan Army will suddenly succeed in now the eighth year of the insurgency. Afghans need no real training to fight. They are not culturally inclined to membership of formal standing armies and for this reason retention, and even attendance, have been historically poor. Karzai has been comprehensively discredited in the recent fraudulent election, which will be an obstacle to co-opting moderate Afghans. However, recourse to regional Afghan strongmen, formerly labelled warlords, may in fact allow an elegant exit with US and European national security objectives intact, but with development and governance objectives still trailing behind.

Regional Forecasts

Africa

In 2010 there will be a marked increase in the presence of non-Western oil and gas majors in Nigeria's energy sector, with Gazprom expected to begin several gas related projects. The entry of Russian and possibly Chinese operators will provide **Nigeria**'s government, which plans to overhaul the organisation and regulation of its petroleum sector, with alternative partners. This, in addition to plans to increase participation of Nigerian-owned companies, will heighten expropriation and contract frustration risks for Western oil majors. More stringent local employment and service provision laws are expected, in addition to greater enforcement of rules requiring vessels operating in Nigerian waters to be locally owned and operated. Major tankers engaged in international transfers are unlikely to be affected. However, Nigerian maritime operators are increasingly likely to detain and obstruct smaller vessels transporting petroleum products.

Production from **Ghana**'s Jubilee oilfield is currently scheduled to begin in the final quarter of 2010, relieving pressure on government finances. Oil processing capacity is likely to be increased significantly by improving efficiency at the existing Tema Oil Refinery and the building of a 200,000 barrel per day (bpd) refinery in Accra by South Africa's New Alpha. Exploration efforts are set to intensify in blocks off **Liberia**, **Sierra Leone** and **Côte d'Ivoire** in 2010. If the finds prove commercially viable, this is likely to stimulate efforts to implement a common maritime security policy for West Africa, aimed at countering militant and pirate attacks on energy assets and vessels. Leading participants will probably include Nigeria, Ghana and Cameroon, aided by equipment and training from France and the US.

President Camara of **Guinea** hopes to transform his military government into a civilian one with elections in 2010. The operating environment is likely to be tougher for mining companies whether Camara emerges as president or not. Most existing contracts signed with Camara's predecessor are opaque and Guinea's next president will be under union pressure to rebalance them towards the government. Companies not suffering expropriation will probably see higher taxes, more requirements to invest in local development and more stringent environmental and labour laws.

In **South Africa**, we expect that the need to reassure foreign investors, combined with fiscal constraints, will limit any dramatic swing to the political left. Jacob Zuma's African National Congress (ANC) government will, however, increase efforts to address poverty and job losses, especially in manufacturing. In April 2009, the ANC said it planned accelerated land reform but not expropriation of farms. Zuma has also affirmed the government's goal of placing 30% of land in the hands of the rural poor by 2014. The government is creating a state mining firm and is likely to give it preferential treatment compared to private mining companies. In this way, the government aims to boost its revenues from the sector, rather than nationalise mining assets. Organised labour and a large section of poor black South Africans are likely to launch extensive protests over working conditions and social services provision in the run-up to, and during, the FIFA World Cup in June/July 2010.

Zimbabwe's Movement for Democratic Change (MDC) is likely to become increasingly frustrated over continued violations of the Global Political Agreement (GPA), which led to the establishment of the unity government. These include ongoing violent farm invasions, the appointment of Zanu-PF loyalists, such as the Central Bank governor and attorney general, arrests and attacks on rights activists and the unwarranted delay in swearing in MDC cabinet nominees. Moreover, the MDC is likely to fight with Zanu-PF over drafting the new Constitution, a central aspect of the GPA. However, given the extent of the MDC's involvement in the unity government, rather than withdraw, the MDC is more likely to refer such violations to the Southern African Development Community (SADC), the guarantor of the GPA, for mediation.

General elections are tentatively scheduled for 2010 though these are unlikely to be free or fair. If they do threaten to increase the MDC's power significantly, there is a mounting risk Zimbabwe's military establishment will intervene, fearing retribution and the loss of its corruptly acquired property. President Mugabe's removal from office, whether through death or resignation, or indeed a perception he is losing control, would heighten the risk of a military coup or sudden revolt by hardliners within his party.

We expect **Angola**'s President dos Santos to run in and win presidential elections in 2010. He is likely to keep his ambitious economic development agenda on course. However, fiscal pressures and lower foreign exchange reserves will probably mean delays and cancellations for some large energy projects. The September 2009 launch of Chevron's $40 billion Tombua-Landana oilfield is expected to boost oil production capacity by 100,000 bpd by 2011, cementing Angola's status as Africa's largest oil producer.

In central and east Africa, **DRC** President Kabila will move to consolidate his coalition before elections in 2011, increasing government appointments for Parti Lumumbiste Unifie (PALU) party members whose strong Western support base would assist his re-election. In the Kivus and northern Maniema, we are likely to see a new Rwandan-led military operation in 2010 against the FDLR Hutu militia blamed for the genocide. In the far northeast, around Bunia, the Front Congolais pour la Justice au Congo is likely to increase attacks through 2010 while seeking to control artisanal gold mines following the retreat of the Lord's Resistance Army (LRA). For its part, the LRA will probably face another major Ugandan Army offensive.

Through 2010 we expect to see an increase in tribal disputes in **Uganda**, particularly with the Bunyoro over the management of oil wealth in the north. President Museveni will probably announce his intention to run for re-election in 2011, despite widespread opposition.

Local, legislative and presidential elections are due in **Burundi** in mid 2010. Although disarmament and reintegration of the ex-rebels from the Forces Nationales de Liberation (FNL) made significant progress in 2009, excluded rebels are likely to attack police and government assets through 2010, especially in the run-up to elections. Risks will be highest in Bujumbura Rural and in the northwestern border area with DRC.

Power struggles within the grand Kibaki–Odinga coalition in **Kenya** are set to intensify as the number of government ministries is cut from 42 to 24. Several key individuals who planned and orchestrated the 2007-08 post-election violence could well revert to similar tactics if marginalised in this process. Unrest would probably be less intense though with the security services reacting quickly.

Disagreements over elections in 2010 and South **Sudan**'s referendum in 2011 are the most likely triggers for a return to full-scale war (see Sudan: Triggers, Indicators and Realistic Scenarios for Renewed North–South War). Although neither side wants this, both sides are preparing. The north has increased weapons purchases from China, including surface-to-air missiles and fighter jets, while South Sudan has acquired tanks from Ukraine and is trying to create an Air Force. Both sides are also seeking alliances with proxy tribal militias, especially in the oil-rich central areas of Kordofan. In the event of war, Kordofan would be a focus for fighting and we expect oil operations would be forced to a halt for the duration.

The Sudan People's Liberation Movement (SPLM) has been working to increase its nationwide footprint ahead of the 2010 polls, forming alliances with Darfuri groups in the west and tribal and political groups in central and northern Sudan. Any indication President Bashir's National Congress Party is likely to lose elections will make Bashir less inclined to compromise on the disputed census results. President Bashir wants the required endorsement for the South Sudanese independence referendum to be a 70% 'yes' vote. He also wants South Sudanese outside the region to be allowed to participate. The SPLM is unwilling to countenance either condition. Failure to agree would probably result in the SPLM declaring unilateral independence, which, in turn, would probably trigger war.

International naval patrols in the **Gulf of Aden, Indian Ocean** and waters off **Somalia** are unlikely to curb piracy in 2010 and risks to vessels will be severe. The presence of warships does not address piracy's main causes: absence of effective government in Somalia, lack of economic opportunities and widespread availability of arms. Our data indicates that the number of attacks and their success is more influenced by the weather than the number of patrolling vessels, with boardings far more difficult during the monsoons (generally from June to September and December to March). Efforts to increase the effectiveness of anti-piracy naval patrols are likely to focus on clarifying legal procedures surrounding the arrest of pirates and action to prevent boardings. Kenya will probably emerge as the main centre for trying detained pirates. We are not aware any foreign power has indicated significant willingness to launch operations against pirates on land, which would have a much more substantial impact. We gather 50 fields of data against every piracy incident in Somalia, the Gulf of Aden and the Indian

Ocean; please see one of the datasets on successful and attempted hijacks between June 2007 and September 2009 below.

Successful and Attempted Hijacks
01 Jun 07 - 20 Sep 09 *(314 incidents)*

Attempt ■ Hijack

Source: Exclusive Analysis

Asia

The capability of the Pakistan-Taliban has increased over the last year and al-Qaeda's leadership has awarded **Pakistan** a more central position in its global strategy. However, the Pakistani state is unlikely to break up in 2010 or the authorities lose control of the country's nuclear weapons. Fresh elections are not expected as President Zardari seeks to consolidate his improved popularity following the Army's operational successes in Swat. The Army would only consider a military coup if it perceived that national security had deteriorated very significantly. This might be due to a series of large-scale terrorist strikes or prolonged civil unrest, something we deem unlikely in 2010.

India's Congress-led United Progressive Alliance government is likely to be stable throughout 2010, pursuing its economic reform programme under Prime Minister Singh and Finance Minister Mukherjee (see The Politics of

Investment Reform in India). The Congress will probably dilute existing caps on foreign direct investment in certain sectors including retail. Opportunities for foreign infrastructure and telecoms companies in India are likely to increase in 2010 and the tax code for foreign investors will probably be tightened.

Remaining fighters of **Sri Lanka**'s Liberation Tigers of Tamil Eelam (LTTE) have split into autonomous guerrilla groups in the north following their military defeat. The Army, which now controls all territory in the Northern Province, is likely to boost its presence there significantly, building bases in Kilinochchi and Mullaithivu, the former LTTE headquarters. Construction of a new naval base in Chalai, the former Sea Tigers base, will probably be completed in 2010. Despite a substantial erosion of marine capability, we expect sporadic suicide boat attacks on government-chartered ships near the coastline between Trincomalee and Point Pedro. Colombo is likely to be the main aspiration target for Tamil rebels, with hotels, transport assets and government buildings particularly at risk. Attacks on vehicles suspected of association with the rehabilitation programme and military operations along the key A9 supply route from Colombo to Jaffna are expected.

The guerrillas' capability to regenerate a sustained campaign will largely depend on the government's progress resettling some 300,000 internally displaced persons (IDPs), currently held in camps in Vavuniya. Operational constraints with de-mining and interviewing IDPs to make sure they weren't rebel fighters, are likely to slow Tamil reintegration. If Sinhalese political will to implement the Constitution's 13th Amendment (which devolves regional autonomy to the Tamil-majority Northern province in areas such as policing and education) is lacking, recruitment to the Tiger's cause will probably strengthen in 2010.

Elections are due in the **Philippines** in May 2010. Election-related violence, primarily small-scale bombings in Manila and anti-government protests, is likely to increase before elections, especially if President Arroyo seeks another term. (Arroyo is currently not eligible to run, but is pursuing controversial constitutional reforms that could allow her candidacy.) In any event, competition among potential presidential candidates, including Noli De Castro, Francis Escudero, Loren Leguarda and Manuel Villar, is strong. Anti-corruption investigations of investment deals, many of which involve Chinese companies and were facilitated by the president's husband, Miguel Arroyo, are likely in 2010, particularly if the opposition wins the elections. The government's negotiations with the Moro Islamic Liberation Front and the New People's Army are likely to continue in 2010 as Arroyo pushes her peace credentials ahead of the end of her term, but little progress is expected.

In **Indonesia**, the twin bombings of the Marriott and Ritz Carlton hotels in Jakarta in July 2009 indicate a greater dispersal of bomb-assembly capability within Jemaah Islamyiah, and an increase in attack coordination. Attacks on hotels and entertainment venues catering to Westerners are likely over the coming year. President Yudhoyono's re-election has positive implications for contract certainty in the mining sector, as he is less likely to review mining contracts than some opposition politicians. However, many uncertainties regarding the implementation of the new Mining Law remain, particularly regarding divestment, licensing and mineral processing requirements, increasing regulatory uncertainty in 2010.

In **Thailand**, the ruling coalition headed by Prime Minister Vejjajiva's Democrat Party is unlikely to complete its term, which ends in December 2011, given substantial opposition. The government is likely to pursue constitutional reforms that limit the number of democratically elected government representatives, as its urban support base is smaller than that of the rural-backed opposition. We expect reforms to trigger renewed political protests, particularly in Bangkok's government district. Should the opposition return to power, coup risks are likely to increase, given the opposition's alliance to former Prime Minister Thaksin, who was ousted by an Army coup in 2006.

China's government will continue to actively support state-owned enterprises' investments and acquisitions overseas, especially in the natural resources sector. Some key target countries for investment are: Australia, Myanmar, Saudi Arabia, UAE, Libya, DRC, Angola and Sudan. Further efforts to internationalise the renminbi, including expanding the use of the Chinese currency in international trade, are anticipated.

Domestically, China is likely to review its metals sector consolidation strategy, focusing on creating metals subregions rather than cross-provincial mergers. Subregions, such as Northeast (Heilongjiang, Jilin and Liaoning) and North (Hebei, Shandong, Shanxi and Shaanxi), would help reduce inter-provincial rivalry and further the government's goal of industry consolidation. Protests over environmental concerns are also likely to affect foreign metal companies' investments, particularly in Yunnan, Hebei, Shanxi and Shandong.

North Korean leader Kim Jong-Il is likely to focus on ensuring the unchallenged transition of power and ideology to his son Kim Jong-Un. This is likely to take the form of further intercontinental ballistic missile tests, aimed at demonstrating to Kim's opponents and his son that North Korea's military strength is an internationally recognised source of influence that needs to be maintained. Such tests will most probably occur during delays or breakdowns in bilateral negotiations with the US or multilateral talks. Even though North Korea annulled a ceasefire agreement with the South following its second nuclear test, it has very little motivation to initiate a conflict beyond the occasional naval skirmish.

The strong Democratic Party of **Japan** majority in both houses of Parliament will help it push through legislation, including a 25% reduction in greenhouse gas emissions by 2020. The government aims to reduce the power of the bureaucracy, increase social spending and reduce taxes.

Eurasia and Europe

Resumption of war in **Georgia** is a significant risk in 2010 given the unresolved status of Abkhazia and South Ossetia, the forced departure of independent UN and Organisation for Security and Co-operation in Europe observers from the conflict zones and Russia's border defence agreement with the two secessionist regions. Russia wants to remove Georgian President Saakashvili from power and probably calculates military force will be required. Violence will probably be limited primarily to cross-border incidents around the conflict zones targeting security personnel. Rail and road infrastructure outside the two regions, especially in the Zugdidi province, is at particular risk.

Violence will probably intensify around the second anniversary of the war on 7 August and during military exercises. Georgian forces are likely to seize vessels travelling to and from Abkhazia, and Russian forces seize those in Abkhazian territorial waters and in Georgian territorial waters close to Abkhazia. Ships and their cargo will probably be auctioned off and the crews detained and tried. Aviation assets most likely to be attacked are unmanned aerial reconnaissance vehicles and Russian military aircraft across or near Georgia's borders with the secessionist regions. Aircraft carrying government officials face a significant shoot down risk. The risk to ground assets in Georgia proper, including Tbilisi airport, would increase only with a return to large-scale fighting.

After the **Russian** government's initial large-scale support for banks, the authorities are becoming increasingly selective in providing state funding to private banks. New legislation will likely be adopted allowing the Central Bank to provide funding only to banks with specified minimum assets (currently $1.6 billion). This means that only about 65 of 1,100 banks in Russia could receive state support. In addition, the Russian authorities introduced a minimum capitalisation requirement for Russian banks in April 2009, aimed at fighting money laundering. Banks must have at least $2.6 billion in assets by January 2010 and $5.2 billion by 2012. Even if this threshold is lowered due to ongoing economic weakness, the legislation is likely to stay in place.

Home-grown extremist nationalist groups now pose a greater threat to foreign assets and expatriates in major Russian cities than insurgents from the North Caucasus. All such groups have a racial agenda and target foreigners from Africa, Asia, Central Asia and the North Caucasus. Several such groups have staged attacks in major Russian cities hoping the blame will fall on terrorists from the North Caucasus, in the process discrediting their insurgency. Assets most at risk in 2010 are suburban shopping centres and street markets (where most traders tend to be foreigners), public transportation (including buses and the underground system) and central public squares in Moscow and St. Petersburg.

Ukraine is due to hold presidential elections in January 2010. The two principal contenders are Prime Minister Yulia Timoshenko and Viktor Yanukovich. In the run-up to elections, business figures associated with Yanukovich, such as Dmitri Firtash and Rinat Akhmetov, will face considerable nationalisation and licence cancellation risks for their financial and natural resource interests. However, if Yanukovich wins the presidency in January 2010, as opinion polls predict, any such actions will probably be reversed. Non-payment and default risks are also likely to increase, with Ukraine's economy depending heavily on IMF funding. Prime Minister Timoshenko's government has been reluctant to follow the IMF's loan conditionality and reforms will likely be postponed with political infighting following the poll. This increases the risk that the IMF will delay releasing subsequent loan tranches. This would considerably increase non-payment risks for state-controlled companies, including energy firm Naftogaz Ukrainy and domestic banks. Major subsidiaries of foreign banks will likely stay afloat given infusions from mother companies continue.

There is very likely to be significant investment opportunities across new European Union members in **Central Europe**. Several countries are struggling with shrinking economies and rising budget deficits, especially the three **Baltic states** and **Hungary**. As a response, the governments are proposing large-scale privatisation programmes to attract foreign direct investment and improve state finances. Investment opportunities emerge both in 'strategic sectors', including energy, chemical and aviation industries, as well as in banking and other services. **Poland** will embark on the largest privatisation programme with some 740 state-controlled enterprises for sale, including the country's second largest refiner Lotos, as well as power providers Enea and PGE. The authorities plan to raise some €10 billion. **Romania** plans to bring in €4 billion with proposed asset sales including military aircraft producer Avioane Craiova and pharmaceutical firm Antibiotice. Privatisation will likely accelerate in **Hungary** after general elections in April 2010. Investment opportunities will open up primarily in postal services and highway construction. The risk of re-nationalisation or asset confiscation following privatisation is limited in these EU members. However, local governments are likely to oppose the increasing presence of Russian interests, especially in the energy sector, given the region's already significant dependence on Russian gas and oil supplies.

General elections have to be held in the **UK** before June 2010 with a Conservative Party victory probable. Any government will have to reduce a budget deficit projected to reach 12% in the current fiscal year. Cuts to expensive military expenditure such as the aircraft carrier project and the renewal of the Trident nuclear weapon system are expected, as are cuts to welfare budgets.

Dissident Republicans in **Northern Ireland** have acquired sophisticated bomb-making skills, most likely by recruiting former members of the Provisional Irish Republican Army (PIRA). Their aim is to provoke an increased security presence on Northern Ireland's streets by killing police officers and members of the armed forces. This strategy makes targeted shootings and low-level car bombings in Northern Ireland much more likely than on the UK mainland. Given Sinn Fein's political weakness, and the impression among some Northern Irish citizens that the Executive is 'not working', dissident Republicans will try to exploit this political discontent unless security forces manage to arrest and disrupt cells. Such disruption is likely given intensified intelligence efforts in Northern Ireland.

In **Germany**, violent protests by left-wing activists including fighting with the police and looting of shops have become a regular occurrence in several cities, especially Hamburg and Berlin. These protests typically involve some 1,000 activists, set on injuring the police and damaging property. With reports of attacks relayed on websites inspiring more such activity, it is increasingly likely that a small group with more significant capability will emerge in 2010, placing explosive devices and carrying out arson attacks.

Greece's Socialist PASOK party won the October 2009 elections with a clear majority. Industrial unrest will probably decline as PASOK is more sympathetic to unions than its predecessor. Terrorism risks, however, will decrease only if the police successfully infiltrate and arrest left-wing terrorist groups, such as Revolutionary Struggle, who are currently staging attacks with explosive devices up to car bomb size.

Americas

In the **US**, President Obama's popularity is suffering from attempts to transform health care and implement energy policy reform. This could cost the Democrats 20–35 seats in the 2010 mid-term congressional elections, though they will probably keep overall power (Republicans need to capture 40 to retake the majority). However, this will leave Obama dependent upon retaining support from conservative 'Blue Dog' Democrats. They often lean far right on social and economic issues like business regulation, tax cuts and labour rights. Furthermore, to protect his right flank prior to the 2012 elections, Obama is likely to shift right on a number of matters post 2010. These include tax relief for individuals and companies and social issues such as abortion. Congress is likely to modify heavily the administration's plan to pass cap-and-trade legislation on climate change. The legislation will probably provide lenient standards for coal and gas producers, given objections from powerful senators from Appalachia, the west and the south.

The left-wing tide prevalent in Latin America in recent years is likely to reverse partially, with centre-right parties expected to come to power in **Chile**, **Uruguay** and **Brazil** in 2010. Furthermore, governments that have embraced radical left agendas, such as those in **Ecuador**, **Bolivia**, **Nicaragua** and **Venezuela** are facing a myriad of domestic challenges. Venezuela's President Chavez has used 'oil diplomacy' in recent years to make inroads in Central

America and the Caribbean. Budget pressures will, however, seriously curtail this in 2010. Chavez's inability to garner enough support to restore to office his close ally, deposed Honduran President Manuel Zelaya, demonstrates his limited international influence.

Despite significant macroeconomic distortions and cash flow problems, Chavez is likely to deepen his 'Bolivarian socialism' in 2010, increasing state control of oil service and petrochemical firms, food manufacturing and distribution and rural estates (see Chavez's Vision: Workers Councils and Upcoming Nationalisations in Venezuela). Workers Councils will be encouraged to take control of private businesses, with Community Councils (controlled by Chavez) given increasing powers to manage public money and have the final say on issues such as the provision of education, health, water and electricity. Most state-run companies, including oil firm PDVSA, face serious cash flow problems, causing job cuts and long delays in salary payments. Budgetary pressures are forcing the government to cut spending for food, health and education. This is frustrating government supporters and raising civil unrest risks.

In **Colombia**, the consistent downward trend in the number of terrorist attacks, kidnappings and murders stalled or even reversed in 2009. Drug trafficking gangs formed from former right-wing paramilitaries will probably become more heavily involved in extortion-related bombings in 2010. 'Plan Rebirth', launched by Alfonso Cano, the FARC's top leader since April 2008, will see a smaller organisation (perhaps a quarter of its 16,000 fighters a decade ago) but with more ideologically dedicated members and a stronger urban presence.

The FARC is likely to step up sabotage against electricity towers and oil pipelines (especially the Trans Andino pipeline) and attacks on security forces around presidential elections in May 2010. Attempts to detonate car bombs against government and security force buildings in Bogotá are likely. The southwestern provinces of Cauca, Huila, Nariño and Putumayo, plus southern parts of Valle del Cauca and Tolima, are likely to experience the most violence. Any incidents of Colombian security forces straying across borders, or airspace violations by US military aircraft based in Colombia, could well result in limited armed skirmishes with Ecuadorean or Venezuelan armed forces. This is especially the case if former Defence Minister Juan Manuel Santos is elected Colombian president.

If current trends continue, **Peru** could overtake Colombia as the world's biggest cocaine producer by 2011. The remnants of the Shining Path guerrilla group are latching on to booming drug revenues to regain strength after near annihilation in the 1990s. Most Shining Path attacks are likely to be focused against security forces in rural parts of Junín and Ayacucho provinces, but also occasionally in Cusco, Huancavelica, Huánuco and San Martín. However, as April 2011 elections approach and the military steps up its counter-insurgency efforts, the Shining Path is likely to attempt a limited number of high-profile attacks, probably targeting government buildings in provincial capitals like Ayacucho or Lima.

Indigenous groups in the Peruvian Amazon will probably persist with their campaign against natural resource exploration and mining on their ancestral lands, especially in Cusco, Loreto, Ucayali and Amazonas (see Protests in Peru: The Outlook for Natural Resources Investors). Oil pipeline pumping stations, hydroelectric facilities, oil and gas fields and electricity distribution are all targets for occupation. The risk of property damage would increase if the police adopt a heavy-handed approach. Indigenous groups in highland areas are likely to step up their disruptive protests against mining, which can include denying access to mines for several weeks. These will probably be most prevalent in Cajamarca, Ancash, Cusco and Ayacucho.

President Morales of the Movement Towards Socialism party in **Bolivia** is almost certain to win a second four-year term in December 2009. Opposition attempts to block enactment of the 2009 Constitution increase the likelihood Morales will bypass institutions and govern by decree. Plans to grant autonomy at regional, provincial and municipal levels will coexist with a recognition of Indian customs as law, generating a confusing legal environment for investors. Increasing political polarisation and racism between pro- and anti-Morales groups is likely to lead to violent confrontations and vandalism of state entities in the eastern lowland provinces. Using accusations of sedition, the government will periodically attempt to break the economic base of the lowland agri-business elite. Moves towards nationalising railways and the electricity sector are anticipated.

In **Mexico**, the September 2009 dismissal of the attorney general indicates the Calderón government is preparing to intensify its three-year offensive against the drug cartels. Given the strength of the inter-cartel war for domination of routes, drug-related killings are not expected to fall notably (see Behind the Headlines: Violence in Mexico and Central America). Mexico will probably accept discrete but increasing US counter-narcotics cooperation. Partly due to increased pressure back home, Mexico's drug cartels are expanding their presence in Central American states, especially **Guatemala**, where their growing penetration of political and security force structures is increasing homicide and kidnapping risks in the country. With more drugs now remaining inside these transit countries, violent disputes between rival gangs result in some of the world's highest homicides-per-capita rates. **Honduras**, which is likely to face regular protests and small-scale bombings by those refusing to accept the military ousting of President Zelaya in June 2009, stands out in this regard.

The defining issue in **Brazil** in 2010 will be the presidential elections and who will succeed Lula da Silva. Lula is endorsing his chief of staff, Dilma Rousseff, as his heir apparent, though many in his party resent the way he has done this. With Rousseff lagging in the polls, the door is open for Sao Paulo governor, Jose Serra, leader of centre-right party PSDB. Brazil is therefore likely to elect a centre-right government, more at ease with pro-business policies and willing to undertake the pension, tax and labour reforms long postponed by Lula. Under a Serra presidency, nationalist tendencies, currently expressed in oil policies and support for national champions, are likely to be reined in. As Brazil has emerged quickly from recession, prospects for strong growth in 2010 and 2011 have improved significantly.

In **Argentina**, a bitter confrontation with the farmers and loss of the mid-term congressional elections have severely weakened Cristina Fernandez de Kirchner's government. Increasingly desperate measures have been employed to avoid debt default, including nationalising private pension funds. With about $20 billion worth of government debt due to be paid in 2010, the risk of another sovereign default is considerable unless lines of credit are secured from the IMF. This is looking increasing likely as the new finance minister now appears ready to talk to the IMF and to holders of previously defaulted debt.

Middle East

An ongoing split between **Iraqi** parties advocating strong central government and those seeking maximum power for the regions is likely to mean limited progress on unresolved legislative issues. This includes the Hydrocarbons Law, and amendments to the draft Constitution of 2005, including article 140, which sets out a timeline for a census, in addition to other articles relating to the power of the regions vis-à-vis the central government. Political risks for foreign oil companies entering Iraq will therefore be significant as a regulatory framework is still likely to be lacking. For oil companies in Iraq's Kurdish region, the risk of being prevented from bidding for contracts in the rest of Iraq by the government in Baghdad is considerable. The Iraqi government considers contracts signed by the Kurdish regional government (KRG) after 2007 as illegal.

Meanwhile, KRG pressure for a census to resolve the status of the so-called disputed territories in northern Iraq (which it seeks to incorporate into the Kurdish Region) will likely sustain frequent bombings and assassinations in 2010. These will target respective Kurd, Turcoman and Arab communities in the mixed cities of Mosul and Kirkuk.

Following a military operation in Basra against militias in 2008, a marked breakdown of security in southern Iraq is unlikely. A key indicator will be the maintenance of a ceasefire by Shia leader Muqtada al-Sadr on the activities of his Jaish al-Mehdi militia. Also crucial will be the government's ability to negotiate ceasefires with other active Shia militias, as occurred in August 2009 with the Asaib al-Haq group.

The maintenance of an overall reduction of violence in Baghdad and central Iraq will, to some extent, depend on the Iraqi government's willingness to provide jobs for the Sons of Iraq (SoI) neighbourhood groups. These comprise former insurgents and Sunni tribes that turned against al-Qaeda. However, the Shia dominated government, still fearful of a Baathist revival, deeply mistrusts the SoI, whom they perceive as disloyal. This is likely to undermine the prospects for national reconciliation and increase the risk that SoI groups will offer their support to the insurgency.

Across the **Gulf Cooperation Council (GCC)** and especially in **Dubai**, we expect project cancellations and construction delays amid a weakened property market, though on a somewhat lesser scale than in 2009. A serious drop in the oil price, and hence state revenues, would intensify this risk.

Saudi Arabia has seen defaults worth at least $15 billion by two large, well-established family conglomerates – Saad Group and al-Gosaibi. Previously, such well-established family firms had ready access to credit based on their reputation and history in Saudi Arabia. Significantly, the Saudi government has refused to bail out either Saad Group or al-Gosaibi, and has frozen the personal and family assets of billionaire Maan al-Sanea, Saad Group's chairman.

The state's refusal to rescue either is likely to make regional banks still less willing to lend to large, Gulf-based firms. It is also likely to curb significantly the practice of 'name-lending' (lending based on family reputation). The decrease in credit availability will probably drive more large family firms in the Gulf to default on loans to regional banks, which are themselves highly leveraged to regional property markets. Strong state support greatly reduces the risks that the region's banks will collapse however.

Kuwait is likely to see political infighting between the royal family and Parliament that will obstruct foreign investment and drive project delays and cancellations, including in the energy sector. This is particularly the case for the technically challenging northern oilfields. **Bahrain**'s concentration on financial services makes it especially vulnerable to the liquidity crisis and regional firms' bad debts. However, Bahrain's relatively capable and influential Central Bank makes it the GCC state most likely to enact meaningful reforms to improve its financial sector's transparency.

Despite dissent amongst **Iran**'s political elite following the presidential elections in June 2009, solid backing from the armed forces suggests the conservative faction, led by Supreme Leader Ayatollah Ali Khamenei and President Mahmoud Ahmadinejad, is likely to retain institutional political power (see Iran: Balancing the Pressures). However, the conservatives will be split internally, with the 'traditionalist' faction that is informally headed by Parliament Speaker Ali Larijani attempting to assert its position vis-à-vis Ahmadinejad supporters. Both conservative sub-factions will, however, strive to keep the reformists out of power. Municipal elections will be held throughout Iran in 2010 for city councils. These will probably test popular support for the president, though reformists could well boycott amid a low turnout.

Iran meanwhile incurs the risk of further UN sanctions. Russia and China are likely to continue opposing sanctions that would significantly impact their own economic interests in Iran, most notably in the nuclear and arms sectors. Any breakthrough in the impasse between Iran and the West on the nuclear issue hinges on major US concessions regarding Iran's uranium enrichment. One scenario might be creating an international consortium to produce uranium within Iran.

Iran will actively attempt to pursue its trade relations with the West throughout 2010, in order to modernise its fledging oil infrastructure and equip itself with the refinery installations necessary to exploit its substantial gas reserves. Parliament will probably push through legislation relaxing restrictions on foreign investment and ownership.

Civil war risks are modest in **Lebanon** in 2010 as no domestic rival can challenge Hizbullah militarily. However, sporadic fighting is highly likely to lead to some casualties and property damage to party offices and affiliated media facilities. A Hizbullah–Israel conflict grows more probable in late 2010-11, as Israel's multi-tiered ballistic missile defence system comes online.

Hizbullah successfully killing or kidnapping Israelis, or attacking Jewish assets, outside Israel proper would almost certainly trigger an Israeli attack on the group and Lebanon's infrastructure. Hizbullah acquiring advanced anti-aircraft weaponry would probably also initiate an attack, though probably more modest in scale.

The risk of assassination of majority politicians will increase if the UN Tribunal for the killing of Prime Minister Rafiq Hariri names Syrian political figures or Hizbullah members as suspects, the latter being more probable. Western military and economic aid will be forthcoming and no significant regulatory changes in the financial sector are expected, though political infighting looks set to obstruct privatisation in the telecoms and power generation sectors.

Yemen faces several threats including a probable war with al-Houthi rebels in the north, a growing insurgency by al-Qaeda in the Arabian Peninsula (AQAP) and a moderate risk of fighting in the south, amid renewed calls for secession. The military will probably use airstrikes, artillery and armour against al-Houthi positions in Saada province in 2010. However, this is unlikely to achieve a decisive military victory or result in a negotiated settlement. A military coup could well depose President Saleh if key political and tribal figures support southern secession, or if renewed violence in the south coincides with an outbreak of serious fighting against al-Houthi.

2. Global Risk Outlook: Global Jihad in 2010

In contrast to many others, Exclusive Analysis assesses that core al-Qaeda ended 2009 in a stronger position than it began the year in terms of its ability to target the West, against which the group is under pressure to prove it can still deliver large-scale attacks. Core al-Qaeda has worked hard to build relationships with Pashtun tribal leaders opposed to US drone strikes in Pakistan's tribal areas and with Kashmiri and Punjabi militants who resent Pakistan's US alliance. Core al-Qaeda is likely to try to exploit networks and contacts belonging to these Pakistani allies to conduct coordinated attacks in the West.

We are likely to see a strong al-Qaeda preference towards recruiting new converts to Islam for such attacks, or using people from ethnic profiles different from those of previous would-be attackers. The **US** will still be the preferred target. However, a successful catastrophic attack is more likely in **Western Europe** in 2010, given the still-limited capabilities of US home-grown militants and the problems externally directed cells face in gaining access to the country. EA's Global Jihad Analysis team assess that the top targets are transport systems and government buildings. Also, although it has not yet featured as a key tactic, we note a number of plots that involved discussion of assassinations. For instance, in the Sauerland case, trial transcripts show that the initial plan was to assassinate senior officials. Likewise, transcripts in the Vinas case suggest that training camps covered kidnapping and assassination training.

US unmanned drone attacks have depleted al-Qaeda's senior leadership in **Pakistan**'s tribal areas. However, although external pressure on the tribal areas has killed key militants – though few key al-Qaeda planners – this very pressure has reduced inter-tribal feuding as the tribes cooperate in the face of an external threat. And it was inter-tribal feuding that made the whole of the Federally Administered Tribal Areas (FATA) such a dynamic and therefore risky operating environment for core al-Qaeda. Now as long as they can avoid US drones and areas of surveillance (and in the relative vastness of the mountains and tribal areas these specific areas are quite limited) then they can hide and plan more easily.

Asia

Despite significant popular support for military operations there, **Pakistan**'s Army and wider security forces are unlikely significantly to reduce the operating capability of militant groups in Pakistan (see the article Pakistan in 2010: New Alliances, New Risks?). Therefore, in 2010 there will probably be an increase in terrorist attacks across Pakistan, especially as militant groups within FATA and groups operating in FATA, Kashmir and Punjab increase tactical cooperation.

India's major cities are at particular risk of attack from Pakistan-based militants. Hotels, government buildings, public places and transport infrastructure in India's major cities are at particular risk of large-scale bomb attacks and armed assaults from Pakistan- and Kashmir-based militants. This is due to their proximity and the militants' wish to trigger an Indian military response. Such a response would almost certainly lead Pakistan's Army to redeploy counter-insurgency operations from the tribal areas to address any perceived Indian threat.

At the time of writing, President Obama is in the midst of a review of US strategy in **Afghanistan**. General McChrystal, commander of the International Security Assistance Force (ISAF), and the Joint Chiefs of Staff, are advocating an enhanced counter-insurgency programme to protect Afghan civilians in population centres. This would require additional troops and almost certainly mean more military casualties. Conversely, Vice President Biden supports a counterterrorism strategy focused on special forces operations and airstrikes in Pakistan, as well as a reduction of US troops in Afghanistan.

In an effort to appease the US military, address declining congressional support for the war and protect his re-election chances in the face of an increasingly unpopular conflict, President Obama is likely to adopt a combination of recommendations from both sides. Such a strategy will probably include the concentration of US forces in Afghan cities and increased efforts to expand and accelerate training the Afghan Army and the police (both necessary for a secure withdrawal). However, low retention of trained personnel risks delaying the transfer of prime responsibility for security to the Afghan government, and hence any exit strategy.

While coalition troops have had some success establishing safe zones in the south and east of Afghanistan (see the article Afghanistan: 360º Strategic Risk Review), militants' operational capabilities are unlikely to be significantly reduced. Increasing distinctions in tactics, leadership and ideology between the eastern and southern insurgencies will probably make counter-insurgency and dialogue efforts less effective. The drug-funded independence of local Taliban commanders, especially in the south, means that any counter-insurgency gains in the east will be less relevant in the south and vice versa.

All that said, we presently see almost no connection between the military campaign in Afghanistan and US and European domestic security. Certainly, there is no evidence of skill transfer to jihadists who would mount attacks in the UK and it is unclear why Afghanistan is any more attractive as a safe haven than, say, Somalia or Sudan.

In 2010, there is likely to be a broadening of the jihadist target set to include non-Western powers that are building a commercial presence in the Muslim world (e.g. Russia, India and particularly China). This will have less to do with solidarity with Uyghur or Caucasus Muslims and more to do with the perception that foreign direct investment by these states helps prop up secular governments that the jihadists deem illegitimate.

Africa

In **Somalia**, some infighting within al-Shabab is likely between those who have purely nationalist ambitions and those who favour a closer alignment with the international jihadist movement, following al-Shabab's declaration of allegiance to al-Qaeda in September 2009. Some members are likely to break away from their hardline Islamist stance in favour of securing a future place in the government. However, more radical elements in the group, including foreign volunteers from the Somali diaspora, will likely attempt at least one terrorist attack across the border in **Kenya**. A suicide vehicle bomb attack against tourist hotels, government buildings or transport hubs is likely. Risks will be highest in the North Eastern Province and the port city of Mombasa, both of which have significant Somali populations. Similar assets in **Ethiopia** and **Djibouti** are also at heightened risk of jihadist attack in 2010, although there are a smaller number of attractive targets for terrorists.

Algerian-based al-Qaeda in the Islamic Maghreb (AQIM) is likely to attempt a major bombing in Algiers in 2010, with hotels, government buildings, embassies and foreign oil company headquarters the top targets. At the same time, the group will be under increasing pressure from the core al-Qaeda leadership to prove its credentials as a pan-North African group. It is particularly likely to engage in attacks in **Mauritania**, where the new government has planned a joint counterterrorism offensive in the border area with Mali and Niger that will target jihadists. French companies will be particularly at risk, with foreign personnel facing a greater threat of attack or kidnap. Indeed, following a suicide attack on the French Embassy in the Mauritanian capital, Nouakchott, on 8 August 2009, AQIM published a statement warning Mauritanian President General Ould Abdel Aziz and his ally, France, that his promised crackdown on jihadist militants would not go unpunished. The likelihood of attacks being staged in Mauritania also grows as AQIM is squeezed in northern Algeria, its main base of operations. State control is, however, lacking on Mauritania's northern border, enabling it to become a staging area for kidnapping, extortion and AQIM activity.

Middle East

Al-Qaeda in the Arabian Peninsula (AQAP), based in **Yemen**, is increasingly likely to employ techniques of suicide bombing and car bomb attacks in Yemen. Foreign energy sector workers are particularly likely kidnapping targets, especially off-site in areas like al-Jawf, Hadramaout and Marib provinces. AQAP is likely to attempt attacks in **Saudi Arabia**, undermining progress Saudi authorities have made in countering terrorism in the kingdom (see the article Reintegrating Radicals: Comparing Results in Egypt, Saudi Arabia and Yemen). While the previous terrorist campaign in Saudi Arabia between 2003-06 concentrated on attacks against energy facilities and foreign personnel, in 2010 we are also likely to see attacks on individuals associated with the Saudi state. A major terrorist breach of Saudi energy facilities, however, still looks unlikely unless AQAP succeeds in obtaining insider help.

3. Forecasting the Unprecedented: What is Forward-Looking Data?

This article considers the relative roles of forward-looking data and historical statistical data in political risk analysis. Rather than compare the wide range of risk-rating and forecasting methodologies available, we focus on the importance and availability of relevant intelligence as inputs for risk forecasting. We illustrate how an intelligence collection plan that incorporated forward-looking data could have forecast the political reversal in Bolivia in 2005 and can help analysts to forecast tactical shifts by terrorist groups. We highlight which information sources most publicly and accurately discussed the probability of a credit crunch before the fact.

The financial events of the last two years, which defied most forecasts, have inspired an explosion in thinking about new methods designed to take into account irreducible uncertainty. For example, in Foresight 2009, Exclusive Analysis outlined some breakthroughs in scenario methods, which have found traction in corporate strategic planning and financial stress-testing. Many scenario methods, however, neglect the question of how to identify the most appropriate data and few are data-driven. In this article, we discuss how to find forward-looking data, which looks for indicators and signals of how imminent an event is, rather than look for patterns in historical data.

Traditionally, a social scientist who wants to forecast the future begins by looking to the past to discern the frequency of many types of events. Assuming that there is abundant data on the particular issue at hand, analysts can identify the underlying conditions in place when the data-event occurred and also assess how closely different sets of data-events correlate with each other. Then, by comparing historical and current conditions, the analyst extrapolates in order to forecast future conditions. In the past 50 years, this statistical approach has made its way from the natural sciences to the social sciences, and today forecasters in most fields are required to use historical data analysis in order to demonstrate rigour.

There are well-known limitations to this approach. For example, identifying which factors are historically correlated (through regression analysis) does not definitively identify which is a cause and which is a consequence. This means that analysts may announce an imminent trend they have not yet seen, because they have identified another trend which (historically) has typically accompanied it. Forecasts derived from statistics may also miss important, and difficult to quantify, social and economic nuances. Alan Greenspan made this point in reference to risk-management models, writing in the Financial Times in March 2008 that models may fail to capture "the innate human responses that result in swings between euphoria and fear that repeat themselves generation after generation with little evidence of a learning curve. [...] This, to me, is the large missing 'explanatory variable' in both risk-management and macro econometric models". Further, in the process of aggregating available data, the outlier, anomalous events (precisely those that might be small early warning indicators of a change) are often discounted by design. The use of counter-factuals, indicators that would disprove the trend or the conventional wisdom, is crucial to forecasting. Finally, the biggest problem, as every stock market investor knows, is that the past is not always an accurate predictor of the future.

The first step in political forecasting is to overcome these challenges. The following table outlines several distinctions between forecasting using intelligence indicators and forward-looking data; and forecasting using historical data.

What is forward-looking data?

Forward-looking data can be identified as such by analysts who make use of some key techniques and principles. An intelligence collection plan must identify extensive risk indicators against which new developments can be assessed. A collection plan must explicitly include identification of counter-factuals (evidence that would disprove the analyst's, or the commonly held, assessment). Systemised collection of appropriate data is critical. A diversity of human sources and audit layers helps to protect against bias. An in-depth analysis of open-source reporting in local media can indicate key caveats or exceptions to the rule. Finally, any collection plan must be dynamic; it must integrate lessons learned from past analytical mistakes and at the same time be open to new sources of data, looking most especially for that which diverges from the trend.

Below we present three examples where forward-looking intelligence was more reliable than historical, quantitative data for forecasting political events: first, a reversal of an historical trend, second, attempts to forecast an unprecedented event and third, testing qualitative intelligence data in financial markets.

	Statistical forecasting	Intelligence-led forecasting
	Historical data	Forward-looking data
Data used...	*Shows historical frequency of the event; or of a similar event (proxy)*	*Shows whether key precursors to the event are happening (indicators)*
Best for...	Very frequent, readily quantified risks	Infrequent, less easily quantified risks, and fat tails (more frequent extreme events)
	(traffic accidents, machinery accuracy, petty crime)	*(inter-state wars, hedge fund collapses, government policies)*
Approach...	Analysis through data manipulation; experiments	Analysis through data interpretation; experiments
	Usually large datasets, analysed for patterns and co-occurence	*Usually smaller datasets analysed for relevance and significance*
Techniques...	Time-series, multivariate regressions, Monte Carlo simulations	Coding, counterfactuals, Bayesian networks, morphological models
Legacy...	Economics, physics, materials sciences	Medicine, sociology, military sciences
Outputs...	Quantified	Quantified, semi-quantified, non-quantified

Source: Exclusive Analysis

1. Trend reversal: Bolivia's rejection of neo-liberal reforms

Bolivia's reversal of neo-liberal reforms in 2005 could only have been spotted with forward-looking data. For nearly 20 years, Bolivia had been a model of market-friendly policy-making. The International Monetary Fund (IMF) frequently held up Bolivia as an example of a modern economy. In 2001, with Bolivia meeting virtually every IMF policy target, the Fund wrote: 'Through sound fiscal, monetary and exchange rate policies and a comprehensive program of structural reforms since 1985 (including extensive privatization, financial sector liberalization, central bank independence and recapitalization, fiscal decentralization, trade liberalization and pension reform), real GDP growth averaged 4% a year during the 1990s, as inflation was reduced to low single digits. Foreign direct investment rose above 10% of GDP during the latter part of the decade …'. Bolivia's sound historical political record gave confidence to the Fund's projections of impressive economic growth and robust foreign direct investment in the years ahead (see table below). Credit ratings agencies corroborated this view: Bolivia's sovereign credit rating was downgraded only twice between 1995 and 2005, while its neighbour, Argentina, a similarly prolific reformer, was downgraded nine times (and upgraded twice).

Bolivia	2001	2002	2003	2004	2005
Real GDP (IMF projection)	4	4.2	5.0	5.0	5.0
Real GDP (actual)	1.7	2.5	2.7	4.2	4.4
FDI (% GDP) (IMF projection)	-	-	-	-	5.9
FDI (% GDP) (actual)	-	-	-	-	-3.0

Source: IMF reports, 2001-06

Until 2004, many policy experts and investors were unable to foresee the significant political changes of 2005, with the election of President Evo Morales. His 'Bolivarian revolution' reversed the prevailing trend of liberalisation into an era of government intervention in markets. This kind of change could only be forecast with forward-looking intelligence because historical data about Bolivia would not suggest an imminent major reversal. A correct forecaster would have needed to analyse the positive results achieved by Morales' party, the Movement Towards Socialism, in the general and municipal elections in 2002 and 2004. This data was not abundant or easy to quantify (because it only comprised two events), but it provided an intelligence indicator of a change in political sentiment. The civil unrest that often followed Bolivia's policy agreements with international donors also required analysis. The challenge was to understand which signals were strong risk indicators and which were weak, which depended in this case on understanding key actors and local influence groups. This case also speaks to the fact that current leaders and policymakers are sometimes the least suited to forecast what will happen next in their own countries and institutions. By definition, they are not impartial observers, and they may be inclined to misinterpret the aims and capabilities of their supporters and opponents.

2. Forecasting the unprecedented: New terrorist attack modes

Distinguishing between risk-relevant intelligence and background noise is key for accurately forecasting when, where and how new kinds of terrorist attacks are likely to occur. Use of open-source inputs to forecast attack probabilities requires nuanced analysis of the source. Online jihadist forums are full of references to both intent and capability to carry out attacks, but they are not necessarily reliable indicators. Jihadist leaders similarly often make threats that are not borne out. In addition, historical data can be unhelpful because, by definition, new modes of attack are unprecedented. Absence of precedence does not, however, imply absence of relevant data. For example, one key open-source indicator is how close terrorist plotters have been to carrying out an attack successfully at the time of arrest. A large number of arrests of suspects in the early planning stages may be less risk-relevant than a single arrest of an individual very close to carrying out the attack because this would indicate that the individual(s) had developed a higher capability of avoiding detection. Of course, this assumes that the plotter(s) had not already been under surveillance for some time and allowed or even encouraged, in a sting operation, to pursue the plot. What is instructive in such cases is often not the historical trend but the early indicators of a divergence from that trend or the conventional wisdom. The undetected plot that nearly reaches fruition may indicate new counter-intelligence capabilities among terrorists; the key influential jihadist strategic manual that criticises a particular currently popular attack type may herald a tactical revolution, and the early evidence that a well-known, high-profile leader's threats do not have predictive power may signal a new operational leadership at odds with their predecessors.

With regard to assessing the relative probabilities of different new attack types, it is possible to build a quantitative, forward-looking model. By understanding the technical requirements for an attack, from conception to deployment, one can model the sequence of steps that the successful terrorist group is most likely to follow. For example, to detonate a radiological bomb in a major financial district, a group would first need to decide upon, and concentrate resources on, that attack mode at the expense of other options. They would need to acquire suitable radiological material and smuggle it into the target country undetected. A viable device would need to be constructed and transported to its target undetected. Appropriate current intelligence data can be analysed to determine the likelihood of each step in the sequence being accomplished successfully in turn. By applying Bayes' probability theorem, a forecast based on current, updatable intelligence (such as security improvements at facilities that store radiological materials), yields the probability of the attack happening in a specific time period.

3. Testing the idea: Credit crunch chatter

The idea that intelligence 'chatter' might help to forecast events in financial markets seems unlikely because it would not reflect the detailed market data that traders routinely use to inform their decisions. However, many financial trading strategies are influenced by social exchanges between traders, including lively social discussions, and they may even occasionally outweigh rational financial data in investment decisions. Economic sociologists who study this topic in depth argue that, in low-income countries particularly, traders often construct market strategies based on local cultural traditions and perceptions. We carried out a study aimed to discover whether there were any non-financial signals in 2006-07 of the impending liquidity crunch – comments in news reports, in banking publications or at corporate events. The risk of a crisis had been publicised by international organisations like the Bank for International Settlements in April and May 2007, but few bodies had much to say about its potential timing.

Our study looked for a wide range of phrases in worldwide news outlets, newswires, press releases, transcripts and company reports between December 2006 and August 2008. The phrases, or 'chatter', incorporated various combinations of terms such as 'economic slowdown', 'credit crunch', 'sub-prime', 'de-leveraging' and 'liquidity bubble'. Various patterns in the chatter were discernible over time. One of the more interesting trends related to how different professions spoke about the possibility of an impending crisis in different ways (we can also see this in data in the run-up to the 1997-98 crisis). We found that deal-makers, usually investment bank brokers, were the most vocal about the credit crunch, as well as the most bearish about credit markets in the run-up to August 2007 (when capital raising by US investment banks intensified). The fact that they act as bellwethers may be unsurprising because brokers are intermediaries and, therefore, have a wider set of interactions and cover a broader range of deals than the counter-parties they bring the deals to. Much like insurance brokers have a wider market view of claims and risk appetite than a single underwriter, brokers in financial markets can acquire a wider knowledge of the types of positions being taken in the market. By contrast, chief executive officers were the least reliable group, consistently underplaying the likelihood of a crisis, arguably because they are so heavily invested in existing plans.

Applying the idea: Some principles

Exclusive Analysis has been built on the principle of professionalising political forecasting with the use of risk indicators, intelligence collection plans, innovative methodologies, layers of audit and supporting infrastructure, as well as a diverse set of professional and cultural backgrounds. Nevertheless, there are some basic and universal operating principles that any political analyst can and should use.

First, it is important to understand the strengths and limitations of each approach in order to choose the right one for the problem at hand. If the choice is simply between statistical and intelligence-led forecasting, then very frequent events can be analysed in much greater detail statistically, and infrequent events involving multiple social actors should be based on forward-looking data filtered through intelligence indicators. In the political sphere, statistical analysis can often yield insightful results, such as revealing patterns in the actions of Somali pirate groups according to local weather conditions, but without an application of forward-looking intelligence that analysis is limited in reliably forecasting future trends.

Second, to ensure that key information is appropriately incorporated, analysts must use an intelligence collection plan that is continuously updated and contains a comprehensive set of questions addressing specific intelligence requirements, based on developing lessons learnt and local contexts. Importantly, these collection plans ensure that new, 'sensational' data (high-profile threats, rocket launches) do not overshadow other less dramatic but more relevant factors or developments. Delivery of correct forecasts requires multiple layers of audit, both internal and external, to discipline both the individual's judgment and avoid 'group think'. Information from human sources should be weighted according to reason-to-believe metrics, such as the source's conflicts of interest, political preferences, degree of risk aversion, competence and access.

Third, integrating counter-factuals into an intelligence collection plan is essential. A good analyst is always looking for any credible evidence that challenges their assumptions, that would make their existing forecast untrue or that would signal a change to a trend.

Finally, the systemised collection of appropriate data and use of precise language around that data is critical to the delivery of correct forecasts. Exclusive Analysis' Country Risk Evaluation and Assessment Model, for example, contains a dataset of over 350,000 risk-relevant events globally. Events are collected, verified and then summarised into single sentences with specific characteristics, such as, for intelligence on violent risks, the event's location, protagonist, target and severity. These form one of the inputs in the forecasting process insofar as they can be used as forward-looking data within the context of intelligence collection plans. Tracking and considering each of these developments in real time is essential to spotting the exception to the rule and to assessing whether the motivations or capabilities of key actors are changing. They can be used to challenge assumptions in a way that a description of the past alone cannot.

4. The Evolution of Economic Warfare

This article suggests that trade sanctions, the most common form of economic coercion, are gradually becoming less effective. This reflects the growth of multilateral trade laws which bar unilateral action; the increasing number of countries that can supply goods and therefore bypass sanctions; moral issues for rich nations following the high-profile human suffering in Iraq and defensive measures available to newly wealthy developing countries. The article highlights alternative methods governments can use to put pressure on other nations, including financial market manipulation and increased influence over global corporations. This piece has broad economic and political relevance, with specific bearing for those dealing with traditional political risk perils such as embargo, contract frustration, confiscation, nationalisation and currency inconvertibility.

Governments have long used trade measures such as tariffs, sanctions and embargoes, as a form of non-military coercion.

Sometimes these trade sanctions have been extremely effective. When OPEC turned the oil taps off in the 1970s in protest at Western policy in the Middle East, the West's energy-hungry economies lurched downwards as oil prices spiked dramatically. Often though, sanctions have proved porous and difficult to enforce. In South Africa, many would argue that sporting isolation was ultimately as influential as any economic sanctions in ending apartheid. During the Cold War, the US and the Soviet Union invariably defied any trade sanctions imposed on their allies. For example, the Soviets supported Cuba in the face of an extreme US embargo. Almost 20 years since the break-up of the Soviet Union and the subsequent collapse in Soviet support for Castro, US sanctions on Cuba have still failed to change the island's political orientation.

Still today, punitive trade measures are often regarded as the best way to try and change a country's behaviour, short of military intervention. For instance, the US and EU favour tightening sanctions against Iran to try to deter it from progressing with its nuclear weapons programme. Venezuela's President Chávez is taking contracts away from Colombian firms, and giving them to Brazilian competitors, in response to Colombia allowing US military bases into the country. Russia regularly uses its energy resources as an aggressive foreign policy tool to put pressure on its neighbours, particularly Ukraine. For example, when Lithuania's government decided to sell the country's major refinery to Poland's PKN Orlen, despite active interest from Russian companies, Russia cut off crude oil supplies to the refinery in favour of alternative export pipelines, primarily via Belarus and the Baltic Transport System.

Over time it has become gradually more difficult to impose effective trade sanctions and this trend is likely to continue.

Since the World Trade Organisation was founded in 1995, trade deals based on the principle of non-discrimination have limited governments' ability to use trade measures unilaterally. Perhaps more importantly though, strong growth rates in developing countries have meant that more nations can now supply raw materials, finished goods, direct investment, skills and know-how. Countries wishing to impose effective sanctions must therefore navigate a wider range of political loyalties than they did in the bipolar world of the Cold War.

Russia still presents challenges for the US in certain foreign policy spheres (e.g. by vetoing sanctions on Iran). Today though, India, Brazil and a whole host of countries are more meaningful players on the international stage. Qatar, for example, can host WTO negotiations in Doha as well as a de facto gas cartel with Russia and Iran. It brokers peace with Hizbullah in Lebanon and hosts US forces destined for Iraq. Newly emerging countries have the power to ignore calls for sanctions on a country, greatly weakening any potential noose and diminishing the often already limited prospects for altering a country's actions.

Clearly the most significant emerging power in this regard is China. For example, the UN, US, and EU have various sanctions in place against Sudan, yet Sudan has been able to use its oil reserves to court investment from China and the UAE, ensuring it is not economically isolated. In May 2007, China rejected new UN sanctions that would increase the number of government officials subject to international sanctions and would expand the arms embargo to the entire country (instead of simply to Darfur). That year, it provided 20% of Sudan's imports, followed by Saudi Arabia, which provided 9%. Chinese companies have also invested heavily in Sudan's infrastructure, such as the Merowe Dam on the Nile and the Quarre I power station near Khartoum, fishing projects in the Red Sea and textile factories in the capital. Despite international sanctions therefore, Sudan enjoyed one of the fastest economic growth rates in Africa, topping 10% in 2006-07, and nearing 7% in 2008.

Furthermore, it has become more politically awkward for developed, economically comfortable countries to push for biting sanctions against a poor country. During the Iraq sanctions experience, ordinary Iraqis paid a very heavy, and high-profile, human price for the sanctions against the country's leadership. This partly explains the desire to move to more targeted measures such as freezing the assets of individuals deemed responsible for the policies.

Developing countries also have some powers to deter the imposition of sanctions. This might most obviously take the form of renegotiating contracts that companies from potentially hostile nations have in that country. In September 2009 for example, there were reports that Guinea was using the threat of expropriation of RusAl's Friguia alumina refinery as leverage to convince the Russian government to block UN sanctions on Guinea's military government.

Many developing countries are now less beholden to economic and financial pressure as a means of coercion.

Considerable debt relief under the Heavily Indebted Poor Countries initiative has eased funding pressures on many developing nations. Furthermore, many resource-rich countries have used a rise in commodity prices in recent years to build up their foreign exchange reserves and pay down their external debt. In Latin America, for example, debt owed to the IMF fell from 80% of the Fund's outstanding loans in 2005 to just 1% in 2008.

Development finance has long come with strings attached. To access assistance, countries would normally have had to tighten their fiscal spending to reduce budget and current account deficits, and tighten monetary policies to rein in inflation. This consistent guidance led to economic policy convergence around the world and a fragile but active consensus in pursuit of free markets, often called the Washington Consensus.

Today, many governments can no longer be swayed by their need to access and service development loans from the World Bank and IMF because they are much less indebted. These governments have far fewer constraints if they wish to delay the creation of free markets, or pursue wholly distinct development agendas. In the case of Latin America, countries such as Bolivia, Ecuador, Venezuela and Argentina have freed themselves from the constraints of IMF debt. 'Liberated', they have gone on to pursue economic policies very different to those which the Fund would have tried to impose on them. Indeed, a desire to sideline the IMF partly motivated a $20 billion capital commitment to the new Bank of the South in September 2009.

Of course, fallout from the global financial crisis has left many nations, especially some in Eurasia (e.g. Latvia, Ukraine and Hungary), in acute economic distress and more heavily indebted to the IMF. It remains to be seen whether some in Latin America, most notably Argentina, will be forced to go back to the IMF for emergency funding in 2010. Overall though, developing countries do look more able to pursue divergent economic strategies. With their debt levels lower and commodity prices in reasonable shape, resource-rich developing nations are driving harder bargains with foreign companies looking to invest.

With sanctions becoming arguably even less useful, are there other ways in which wealthy and powerful countries might seek to 'persuade' weaker nations economically?

Many countries are clearly concerned that hostile nations could use their vast pools of capital for 'political' rather than genuine investment reasons. In 2008, the US and EU adopted bilateral sets of principles designed to help ensure that foreign sovereign wealth funds (SWFs) would not invest for political reasons. These were followed by the global, IMF-sponsored Santiago Principles, developed in consultations. In Foresight 2008, we described some limitations that made SWFs unlikely tools for economic conflict. They are under pressure to deliver returns and are predominantly staffed by finance professionals. Their portfolio investments leave them fairly few tactical options, compared, for example, with a state-owned 'national champion' industrial entity that controls logistical equipment.

However, some governments now have enormous pools of capital at their disposal, and electronic trading systems today are very fast and highly integrated. Should it so wish, China can, for example, threaten to sell all its holdings of Costa Rican government debt unless the latter removes its recognition of Taiwan as an independent sovereign state. It can do this quickly and raise the funding costs for a small country. It can also control timing, waiting for its target country to be in maximum financial difficulty before acting.

Some parties are taking the potential for this sort of hostile behaviour very seriously. In September 2008, Russian President Medvedev questioned whether the US government had some responsibility for the sharp falls in Moscow's stock exchange following Russia's invasion of Georgia. Finance Minister Kudrin put the issue to US Treasury Secretary Henry Paulson.

In April 2009, the US government and several private and non-profit partners ran a war game of economic battles sparked by scenarios in North Korea, Russian gas markets and Taiwan. Under each scenario, the US enacted economic and financial operations that simulated pressure on its adversaries. The facilitation team tallied up potential consequences for other teams (China, Russia, East Asia and others), and these were then given opportunities to respond, as in a conventional war game. One month after this war game, according to US press reports, the US Central Intelligence Agency, traditionally a political animal, launched a recruitment drive for former Wall Street bankers. This was partly to help the Agency identify which economies would be vulnerable to manipulation.

By way of balance, it's important to highlight some factors making it harder to exercise financial pressure of this kind today. Since the Asian Financial Crisis of the late 1990s, many developing countries have built up their stocks of foreign exchange reserves to give themselves larger buffers if attacked. More coordinated defences have also emerged, with many emerging market central banks agreeing to stand behind each other in the event of a currency attack. Many have also moved away from the rigidity of fixed exchange rates.

Governments are more actively lobbying global corporations not to do business in certain countries.

Throughout history, governments have lobbied other countries to try to win trade and investment deals for their national companies. There is also plenty of precedent for governments trying to deter multinational firms from investing in certain countries. For example, the US passed the Iran-Libya Sanctions Act (1996) in a bid to stop US and non-US companies from developing these countries' oil sectors. If anything, this sort of government pressure appears to be strengthening. The US Treasury, for example, now has a dedicated unit to discourage banks around the world from supporting Iranian businesses. It is run by the undersecretary for terrorism and financial intelligence. The unit has persuaded numerous non-US banks, including Switzerland's Credit Suisse and the Netherlands' ABN-Amro, to cut their financing for the letters of credit of Iranian firms and for Iranian state banks like Bank Saderat, in order for them to secure preferential access to Treasury markets. It seems likely that firms expanding into new markets will need to be increasingly mindful of the risks stronger third-party lobbies pose to their investments.

Governments are becoming more involved in economic espionage.

Generally economic espionage is carried out between companies looking for trade secrets, with occasional ad hoc support from their host governments. In the Cold War era, most intelligence collection by governments was of an overtly 'political' nature, and that remains the case today. However, formal intelligence programmes for the protection and collection of sensitive economic information are on the rise. France has one of the leading state-run programmes within its Direction Générale de la Securité Extérieure' (DGSE). Successive directors of France's external intelligence service reported, once retired, that obtaining information from large international companies is a national security priority. Pierre Marion, head of the DGSE under President Mitterand, stated that France would not spy on the US on political matters because they are political allies, but would do so on economic matters because in that sphere they are competitors.

In recognition of the increased role of governments in this sphere, the US Economic Espionage Act, adopted in 1996, allows 'US agencies to investigate cases where a foreign intelligence service, applying traditional methodologies, mounted an intelligence attack against a US company to gather proprietary information to support the commercial interests of a foreign company', according to a US Interagency OPSEC Support Staff report.

Information technology has revolutionised the means for capturing sensitive economic and industrial expertise, and our sources report evidence of economic espionage programmes in several government agencies. Much of it is informal, relying on traditional human networks and interactions between senior corporate executives and intelligence operatives. China, France, Israel and Russia are said to deploy the most intrusive methods, including extensive wiretapping and bribery, particularly in geographies where high-value information combines with relatively low IT-protection capability.

5. Indexing Human Safety: Predictive Indicators for Risks to Personnel

Assessing risk to personnel enables security managers to allocate resources relatively between locations on a data-driven, forward-looking basis. The nature of kidnap and violent attack justifies special treatment and a unique methodology. In this article, through case studies of highly differentiated risk environments, we establish key considerations for strategic security planning and specific evaluation of kidnap and violent risks and the basis on which those considerations would require review.

All violent risks vary by location. However, in contrast to indiscriminate risks to personnel, such as terrorist attacks against hotels, kidnap, detention and targeted assassination are personal. They discriminate on the basis of the nationality, profession, company and association of the target. The incidence of kidnap may be very low in a given location, for example, but for an individual who fits preferred target characteristics, low overall incidence is irrelevant. An individual from a particular mining company may be at great risk in a town where their company has offended locals, but at little risk in a neighbouring region.

Even where accurate historical data is available, it is crucial to move beyond past data in order to assess future risks accurately. Soliciting inputs from local sources who are able to comment on risk indicators based on an understanding of a particular actor or geography is critical. The analysis needs to move beyond the risk of any kidnap or attack happening generally, and the risk of it happening to a specific target set. Analytically, this is the difference between generic frequency and asset/personnel dilution.

Risk indicators are structured definitions of relevant factors to monitor when assessing a risk. They ensure that relevant information for each specific question is collected, while filtering out the irrelevant data. They form a core part of EA's systemised intelligence collection, analysis and audit process. While these multi-tiered indicators are proprietary, a sample selection for Kidnap & Ransom is shown in Table 1.

Predictive Indicators for risks to personnel

EA's Intelligence indicators have been designed to deliver a nuanced analysis of risk of death, of injury and of an individual being deprived of their freedom. The indicators specifically differentiate between threats to nationals, expatriate residents and expatriate visitors. Indicators include risk analysis of:

1) Kidnap. *See Table 1 for further definition.*

2) Discrimination and detention by state agencies

3) Death or injury as a result of war, terrorist attack or violent unrest

4) Losses from organised and petty crime targeting individuals

5) Capability of likely perpetrators of attacks

6) Intent and capability of the state to mitigate these risks

Indicators are only as good as the intelligence collected against them, however. Local sources are crucial for assessing the relative importance of data and specific intelligence. For example, in Russia, the official recorded statistic for kidnappings in Chechnya for the first half of 2009 was 27, whereas non-governmental sources active in the region reported a total of 37. Similarly, in Colombia at least four different organisations deliver different kidnap data of varying quality.

Table 1: Kidnap & ransom indicators

Kidnap & Ransom — selected sample indicators
To what extent could groups that do not currently include kidnap among their tactics acquire a kidnap capability if they changed their strategy?
What are the triggers for such a change in strategy to take place, for example the need to supplement funds to wage an ongoing insurgency?
To what extent do groups assess that an attractive risk-reward ratio for adopting kidnap tactics exists, based on their overall agenda and capability as well as the will and capability of state forces to disrupt them?

Source: Exclusive Analysis Executive Protection methodology

Regional Risk differentiation

Location, statistics and asset dilution

Highly differentiated threat profiles for personnel exist even within single countries. In Nigeria, for example, incidence of kidnap of expatriates is high in the south and relatively low and dispersed in the north. There were only four kidnappings recorded in the north in the first half of 2009, compared to 61 in the Delta states. This is in part a result of the lower numbers of expatriates present in the north, but primarily because the aims and capabilities of the groups active in the Delta make the targeting of expatriates both more likely and more effective. In the Delta states, expatriates are targeted in an attempt to intimidate foreign companies (primarily energy companies) into leaving the area as well as to extort ransom payments from these same companies. The groups also have a geographical advantage in that the creeks in the Delta offer opportunities for hiding hostages that are less present in the arid north. Understanding the geographic differentiation of risk therefore requires both an appreciation of the dilution of assets (in this case, individuals) and the profile of likely perpetrator groups.

This includes careful consideration of: where armed non-state actors have or have had de facto control; security force penetration in these areas; any security force operations in a particular location that may push perpetrators into a new area of operation; the role of topography in the ability of either armed groups or state forces to operate in certain areas; local support for armed groups; and the impact of season and weather on the movement and activities of both armed groups and state forces.

Figure 1: Risk map of Nigeria showing incidents of kidnap and attacks involving explosives

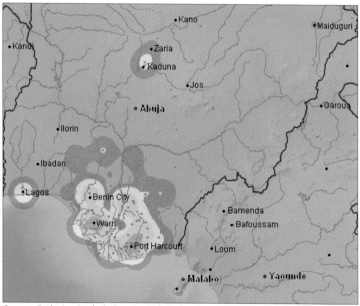

Source: Exclusive Analysis Country Risk Evaluation and Assessment Model (CREAM)

This differentiation of risk applies also to regions within a country, as the breakdown of violent attacks in the Niger Delta states alone over the past 36 months show. Although militants have staged attacks across the Delta states, Rivers State has seen the greatest number by a significant margin. This is the result of a high concentration of attractive targets, including vessels transiting through the Bonny channel to Port Harcourt, energy installations in the area and offices and residences in Port Harcourt. Rivers State is also home to two of the most active militant groups – Ateke Tom's Niger Delta Vigilantes and Dokubu Asari's Niger Delta People's Volunteer Force.

Figure 2: Violent attacks in the Niger Delta by state, Jan 2006 – Sep 2009

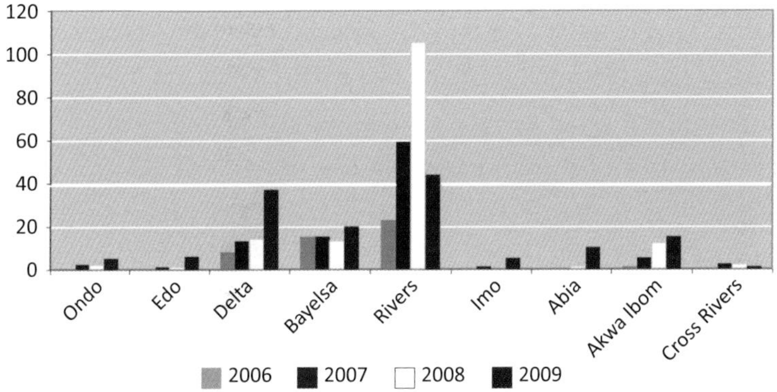

Source: Exclusive Analysis Country Risk Evaluation and Assessment Model (CREAM)

Asset Dilution and Risks to Personnel

Asset dilution is an important consideration in understanding regional differentiation of risks. A lower level of kidnappings or terrorism could be due to concentration of population rather than regionally specific risks. For example, in Colombia, there are more incidents in absolute terms in and around the major cities of Bogotá, Medellín and Calí. However, this partly reflects the fact that there are more commercial and military targets than in the FARC strongholds of southwestern Meta department and Caquetá, for example.

Our risk index takes this into consideration when differentiating between risks to locals and expatriates so that the score reflects not just the risk of something happening, but the risk of it happening to a particular individual (in this case a local as distinct from an expatriate).

Target selection

In addition to geography, victim profiles vary significantly for both kidnap and other violent attack.

For instance, in Lebanon there is clear differentiation between risks to expatriates and to nationals. Whereas expatriates are at very limited risk of kidnap or assassination, Lebanese nationals are at notable risk as incidents of kidnap tend to result from inter-family feuds over property rights or are motivated by revenge for the death of a family member at the hands of a rival family. Assassinations are almost always politically motivated and targeted at active politicians or their patrons.

Again, this is a reflection of the agendas and capabilities of perpetrators as well as the demographics of the area in which they operate. The higher risk of kidnap for locals in Mexico is a reflection of the higher risks involved for perpetrators if they target foreigners as this is more likely to generate a response from foreign security services in addition to the Mexican state; this is particularly the case with involvement by the FBI if US citizens are kidnapped. In Pakistan, the relatively smaller difference in risk faced by expatriates and locals reflects a different dynamic. Most local kidnap victims are targeted as a result of business or criminal disputes, whereas expatriates tend to be targeted by jihadist groups. We expect to see this trend increase over the coming year, making the risk to expatriates only somewhat lower than to locals, even though they are numerically a very small minority in the country.

Figure 3: Comparative risk scores for Death & Injury and Kidnap & Ransom for expatriates and locals

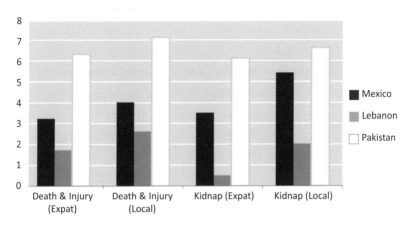

Source: *Exclusive Analysis Executive Protection Index*

Hotspots: Countries of emerging or declining risk to personnel

Accurate risk forecasts give decision makers time to plan against – if not always eliminate – threats. Places where risks can escalate quickly clearly require more detailed monitoring and, particularly, intelligence that delivers warning times that enable effective operational responses. There is less value in receiving a warning on the eve of an attack if the evacuation plan takes three days to activate. Rapid response times might be crucial because of a latent capability of terrorist or organised crime groups, or a long-standing inter-state conflict where troop readiness for war is always kept high e.g. in Israel, Colombia, Georgia or Ethiopia. Systematic monitoring of such indicators allows rapidly increasing risks to be recognised and effectively managed before a situation requires crisis management. For example, Exclusive Analysis maintains indicators and regular horizon-scanning of such key inputs as changes in the capabilities of security services to prevent or respond to incidents (please see the article Behind the Headlines: Violence in Mexico and Central America). Likewise, intelligence streaming on the intent, motivation and leadership of militant groups allows for early identification of changing tactics and target selection (please see Pakistan in 2010: New Alliances, New Risks? and Back with a Bang? Right-wing Extremism in the US and Western Europe).

Selected Case Studies: Kidnapping Risks

In Yemen, specific indicators lead us to expect a significant change in kidnapping trends, namely a lower intent to kidnap and a higher intent to stage attacks with the aim of killing or injuring individuals outright.

Kidnap for ransom is common in Yemen, and the motives for kidnapping expatriates have ranged from ransom or collateral to demanding political concessions. Locals are most frequently kidnapped in attempts to settle disputes over land or marriage. Whereas expatriates have been relatively rarely harmed, kidnappings of locals more often lead to the death or injury of victims. However, the increasing activity by al-Qaeda in the Arabian Peninsula (AQAP) in the Hadramaut and Ma'rib regions is likely to lead to an increase in kidnappings of expatriates that result in victims being killed.

On 22 January 2009, al-Qaeda in Yemen (AQY) announced its merger with AQAP, the al-Qaeda franchise based in Saudi Arabia, under Yemeni leader Nasir al-Wuhayshi, aka Abu Basir. The merger reflects the fact that, as operating conditions have become increasingly difficult for jihadists in Saudi Arabia, some have been displaced across the border. They have probably contributed to the evolution of tactics used by AQY. AQAP's agenda is to eject all non-Muslims from the Arabian Peninsula, prevent non-Muslims from benefiting from the region's oil wealth and overthrow the Yemeni and Saudi governments as a precursor to establishing an Islamic caliphate under sharia law. This agenda is better served by staging attacks resulting in civilian and foreign casualties, as well as by killing hostages rather than negotiating for their release. We therefore expect to see an increase in the execution of kidnap victims by their captors when the responsible group is AQAP, but also for political ransom demands, such as the release of jailed militants. However, this new trend is unlikely to displace kidnapping for financial ransom or to extract concessions from the government, which has been prevalent in Yemen for some time but perpetrated by local tribal groupings rather than militants with a jihadist agenda. The risk of kidnap by tribal militias is greatest in al-Jawf, Shabwa and Ma'rib provinces where they are most likely to target foreigners associated with the energy sector. However, for AQAP, who are mostly active in San'a, Hadramaut and also Ma'rib, all foreigners will be attractive targets.

In Pakistan, we expect jihadist groups, specifically in Karachi, to turn increasingly to kidnap and violent attack on foreigners as well as on wealthy Pakistanis to fund their activities.

In addition, these attacks will serve to intimidate and send a message about these groups' regional and global agenda. To date, the majority of kidnappings in Karachi have been by organised criminal groups looking for ransom (generally targeting wealthy local businessmen) and by political rivals targeting the opposition. There were 92 recorded cases of kidnap in Karachi in 2008, although we understand from our sources that this does not reflect the actual total as many incidents go unreported. For instance, specifically, kidnappings related to business disputes are more likely to go unreported as victims are more likely to simply pay the ransom requested. Kidnap for ransom has also featured significantly in the fundraising activities of the Pakistan-Taliban, notably the Tehreek-e-Taliban Pakistan (TTP) (formerly led by Baitullah Mehsud), who according to our sources, get over 50% of their funds from ransom payments.

In terms of high-profile jihadist kidnapping, the most notable case in Karachi was in 2002, when American journalist Daniel Pearl was kidnapped and subsequently executed by his captors. However, as a result of intensified confrontation between the Pakistan Army and militants in the tribal areas, we expect that jihadist groups are more likely to use kidnappings for ransom as a way to supplement funds and also in order to attract attention with the execution of some hostages. Pakistani militant groups, like the TTP, and the core al-Qaeda leadership (most likely based in Quetta, Pakistan) seek to turn Pakistan into a central battleground for global jihad through attacks that inflict Western casualties. Hotel bombing is one tactic to achieve this aim that we expect to see more frequently, but tactical kidnappings of Westerners (particularly Americans) that end in executions, with the aim of embarrassing the government and deterring foreign investment, are also likely to emerge.

In Cameroon, we expect to see kidnap for ransom become a tactic for secessionist groups in the Bakassi peninsula.

These groups have been learning from militants in the Niger Delta and the prospect of lucrative ransom payments, together with an opportunity to raise the profile of their grievances with the Cameroon government, will make kidnap for ransom an attractive tactic. The groups have shown capability through attacks on Cameroonian soldiers in Bakassi and their subsequent avoidance of capture. They are most likely to target Army posts and public buildings; however, we also expect them to expand their operations to more regularly include kidnappings. In October 2008, a group calling itself the Bakassi Freedom Fighters kidnapped 10 workers of French oil services firm Bourbon from a supply vessel. Reports from our sources suggest that a network of so-called 'resource strugglers' is emerging across the Gulf of Guinea, with aggrieved groups not only on the Bakassi peninsula but as far away as Angola looking to the Niger Delta for training, tactics and weapons. Such collaboration is very likely to lead to a greater frequency of both attacks and kidnappings outside the Niger Delta and particularly in Bakassi where proximity to the Delta will allow militants to move hostages across the Nigerian border if the Cameroon security forces threaten to disrupt their activities.

However, Cameroon has already responded to the threat with more aggressive maritime patrols after several attacks on fishing, energy and other civilian maritime traffic. On 3 August 2009, its Rapid Intervention Battalion reportedly shot at least four suspected Nigerian pirates as they attempted to hijack a fishing vessel. The relatively low concentration of foreign energy companies and staff in Bakassi also suggests that although the risk of both piracy and kidnappings in Bakassi is increasing it is unlikely to reach the scale of attacks in the Niger Delta.

In Colombia, by contrast, the changing nature of the conflict between the government and the FARC guerrilla group will reduce the risk of kidnap.

The FARC has been denied its former secure base areas with a persistent military campaign targeting their senior leadership and bases, which means it is becoming increasingly difficult for the group to manage hostages. Previously, the FARC's bases were well protected and could hold hostages for long periods of time, but when regularly moving locations, hostages become a liability. In addition, new FARC leader Alfonso Cano is more sensitive to the domestic and international public outcry over kidnappings and unlikely to revive the group's previous strategy of kidnapping and holding large numbers of hostages across the country. The deployment of better-trained and more mobile police and Army units, including dedicated battalions for the protection of roads, electricity and energy assets, is also likely to indirectly reduce the number of opportunistic kidnappings in rural areas. Specifically, they make the establishment of FARC roadblocks more difficult.

The Plan Patriot campaign has led to the Ejército de Liberación Nacional (ELN) guerrilla group losing control of its previous strongholds in Santander, northern Tolima and Antioquia, while the FARC has been dislodged from entrenched positions around major cities such as Bogotá and Medellín. Operations Liberty I and II flushed out seven FARC fronts around Bogotá in Cundinamarca and northern Meta, forcing the rebels to regroup in areas of Huila, Tolima and central Meta. Subsequently, Uribe has set up two Joint Commands, which have taken the fight to Caquetá, Meta and Guaviare, and also to the Sierra Nevada. Many guerrillas have been pushed out of Caquetá into southern Putumayo (along the Ecuadorean border), Nariño and (to a lesser extent) Amazonas. The FARC has now sought to retake the initiative along the Ecuadorean border (Putumayo and Nariño), and along the Pacific coast (Cauca and Valle del Cauca), areas which have seen an increase in guerrilla activity. Other areas where the risk level has not fallen with the government operations include Neiva (Huila), Calí and Buenaventura (both in Valle del Cauca). Calí specifically has been the target of several large car bombs, and a FARC offensive in Huila has included several bombs targeting the commercial centre, hotels, Neiva's former mayor and the city's airport.

Top 10 high-risk countries

Country	Overall Risks to Expatriates	Kidnap	Detention	Death & Injury
Afghanistan	5.3			
Somalia	5.2	7.6	0.9	7
Pakistan	5.1			
Iraq	4.9			
Sudan	3.7			
Nigeria	3.6			
Niger	3.5			
Ethiopia	3.2	2.9	4	2.8
Mexico	2.9			
DRC	2.9	1.9	3.5	3.3

Source: Exclusive Analysis Executive Protection Index

6. Agricultural Bioterrorism and Biowarfare: Assessing the Risks and the Consequences

Agricultural assets have been targeted by landless workers movements, indigenous land rights activists and anti-genetic modification protesters. However, unconventional attacks on agriculture (agricultural bioterrorism or 'agroterrorism', utilising pathogens against livestock or crops) have not yet been a tactic of any militant group. Several states have also historically developed biowarfare programmes including agricultural pathogens (some states are likely still to have active offensive programmes, although this cannot be verified), but none have so far deployed them. Natural outbreaks of disease in crops and livestock indicate that costs could run into billions of dollars, with disruption to supply chains, trade embargos and lost revenue, event cancellations, travel restrictions and an erosion of public confidence. Drawing on scientific (biosecurity and veterinary) and political inputs, we consider the likelihood that terrorist groups or states will use agroterrorism as a tactic, which groups might have these aspirations, what their preferred target set would be and which biosecurity measures would mitigate the risk of a successful attack.

To date, agroterrorism incidents have been confined to hoaxes, which have nonetheless caused considerable economic loss and social disruption.

In 1985, a hoax call to the US Embassy claiming that Chilean grapes had been laced with cyanide led to the US, Canada, Denmark and Hong Kong suspending Chilean grape imports, resulting in more than $210 million in export losses. Such an event is indicative of consumer and government reaction to a possible contamination of the food supply. In the absence of previous agroterrorism attacks, naturally occurring outbreaks of contagious disease in livestock and crops such as foot-and-mouth disease (FMD), a highly contagious virus that infects cloven-hoofed animals, and karnal bunt (KB), a fungal disease affecting wheat, provide data for modelling the potential impact of a deliberate attack.

Naturally occurring outbreaks of disease in crops and livestock illustrate the possible multi-billion dollar losses that are likely to result from a large-scale agroterrorism attack.

Each year the agriculture sector in the US alone loses an estimated $30 billion due to crop diseases and $17.5 billion due to livestock diseases. These diseases can be the result of pests and pathogens legally or illegally brought into the country when importing agricultural products, including grain, fresh fruit, meat and live animals. Table 1 highlights some of these pests and pathogens. Developed countries are particularly vulnerable to invasive exotic plant or animal diseases, as these countries usually maintain a 'disease-free' agricultural export status – the highest level of plant and animal health status awarded to countries free of highly contagious agricultural diseases. This status enables free trade of crops, animals and animal products. A single confirmed outbreak can result in trade restrictions lasting a year or more. The effects of an outbreak are wide-reaching, with the UK's 2001 FMD outbreak, in which six million animals were slaughtered across 10,000 farms, causing losses (detailed in Chart 1) to not only farmers but also other rural and agriculture-dependent industries, such as farm-input suppliers, food producers, food-transportation providers, grocery stores and restaurants. Restrictions during the FMD outbreak included road closures and cancellation of public events, with the tourism sector and tourism-dependent industries suffering the most significant losses. In more export-oriented economies a greater proportion of the total losses are likely to be attributed to the loss of food exports. Table 2 details losses caused by major naturally occurring outbreaks globally.

Table 1: Selected Animal Pathogens, Plant Pathogens and Pests

Disease	Endemic Areas	Animals/Plants Affected
Animal Pathogens		
Foot-and-mouth disease (FMD)	Asia, Africa, the Middle East, South America	Cattle, sheep, goats, pigs, wild ruminants
Exotic Newcastle disease	Asia, the Middle East, Africa, Central America, South America	Poultry, wild birds
Rinderpest	East Africa and the Indian subcontinent	Cattle, water buffalo, wild ruminants, sheep, goats, some pig species
Bovine spongiform ecephalopathy (BSE)	Global occurrence	Cattle
Plant Pathogens		
Philippine downy mildew	Philippines, Nepal, India, Laos, Vietnam	Maize
Bacterial wilt or Brown rot	Global occurrence, with the exception of the US and Canada	Potatoes, soybeans
Citrus greening	Asia, Africa, the Arabian Peninsula, Brazil	Citrus fruit
Karnal bunt	India, Pakistan, Afghanistan, Iraq, Mexico	Wheat
Insect Pests		
Asian longhorn beetle	East Asia	Poplar, willow, elm, maple trees
Boll weevil	Central America, Mexico, southern US	Cotton
Whitefly	Predominantly tropics and subtropics	Tomatoes, beans, cassava, cotton, cucurbits, potatoes, sweet potatoes
Russian wheat aphid	Russia, Afghanistan, Iran, US	Cereal crops

Source: Center for Infections Disease Research & Policy, CIDRP, 2009

Chart 1: Key UK 2001 FMD Outbreak Costs ($ billion)

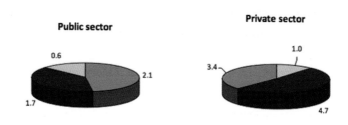

Public sector

Private sector

Source: DEFRA/DCMS joint working paper, March 2002

Table 2: Economic Impact of Naturally Occurring Outbreaks

Event description	Economic impact
Exotic Newcastle disease outbreak, Southern California, US, 1971	$56 million in containment costs 12 million birds slaughtered
Pathogenic avian influenza outbreak, Pennsylvania, US, 1983	$65 million in control costs 17 million birds slaughtered
Foot-and-mouth disease outbreak in pigs, Taiwan, 1997	$4 billion in control costs $15 billion in lost pork exports 4 million pigs slaughtered
Hog cholera outbreak, The Netherlands, 1997	$2 billion in control costs 5 million pigs slaughtered
Karnal bunt identified in wheat seeds planted in Arizona, New Mexico and Texas, US, 1996	$60 million in containment costs $250 million in lost wheat exports
Citrus canker discovered in southern Florida, US, 1995	$200 million in control costs
Foot-and-mouth disease outbreak, UK, 2001	$13.5 billion in losses (see Chart 1) 6 million livestock slaughtered

Source: Center for Infectious Disease Research & Policy, CIDRP, 2009, DEFRA/DCMS, 2002

While some groups have targeted agro-businesses in arson attacks or land seizures, there is no evidence that terrorist groups have planned to carry out agricultural bioterrorism attacks. The primary threat is more likely to come from groups with economic rather than political aims.

The deliberate use of pathogens would be most likely to emerge as a tactic by groups seeking economic advantage specifically through disruption of a competitor or antagonist's livestock or crops or through manipulation of the environment. This risk may arise amid trade disputes or other conflicts in which agriculture is a key issue of contention. One example of economically motivated release of pathogens was the intentional introduction of rabbit calicivirus into New Zealand by domestic farmers who wished to control the rabbit population. After an outbreak in Australia, the New Zealand government outlawed its production but despite this, farmers smuggled in vials of the virus and grew the pathogen using simple kitchen equipment before distributing it. As New Zealand has one of the strictest biosecurity regimes in the world, this case illustrates the difficulty of preventing the smuggling of non-endemic pathogens to a territory.

The concept of economic jihad (targeting assets due to their economic value rather than symbolic or mass-casualty potential) has gained recent support among al-Qaeda leaders and theorists, as well as the movement's rank and file. For instance, the June 2008 strategic document 'Al-Qaeda and the Battle for Oil' discussed the impact of terrorist attacks on commodity prices, and the May 2009 document 'Somalia and the New Treacherous Plan', emphasised economic over military targets in East Africa. This suggests that agroterrorism may in future be viewed as another tactic by which to drain Western economies and to spread panic. Jihadist sympathisers took a keen interest in the outbreak of H1N1 in 2009, with one contributor to the online 'Fallujah' forum commenting in April 2009, 'This new disease... has done more than any human soldier could do, causing damage to morale and terrible financial losses estimated at billions of dollars!' This type of commentary is unlikely to lead directly to an actual plot, but does indicate that the wider jihadist movement is cognisant of the potential of biological attack methods. However, the Islamist worldview of an all-out global conflict between Islam and unbelievers means that agroterrorism is likely to gain interest among Islamists as another potential means of asymmetric attack.

With regard to non-jihadist terrorist groups, the difficulties of delimiting the area affected and of controlling the effects of animal and plant pathogens means that agroterrorism cannot readily be used to attack a specific target to further a narrow political objective – a key motivator for most terrorist groups. We assess that its use by separatist and other terrorist groups who do not have a global agenda is currently minimal. A separatist group that targeted crops or livestock elsewhere in the country could not ensure that their own crops or livestock would not be affected as a result.

There are direct-action single-issue protest groups who may consider agroterrorism as a means of protest against intensive-farming practices, highly concentrated land ownership or the development of genetically modified organisms. They include the Animal Liberation Front (ALF), which operates globally; the Earth Liberation Front (ELF), which mostly operates in the US, and landless workers movements in Brazil, Bolivia and Paraguay. However, they are unlikely to adopt a tactic that would cause widespread harm to animals, the environment and wider economic damage. They are more likely to target the headquarters, vehicles and infrastructure of agri-businesses in conventional attacks, to seize land or to disrupt the movement of goods.

Table 3: Selected Agroterrorism and Agrowarfare Risk Indicators

Probability of attack indicators	Severity of attack indicators
Trade or regulation disputes which leads to organised militant protest movements (e.g. highly disaffected farmers)	Significant dependency on a single crop for food security or export earnings
Weak biosecurity controls at points of entry (airports, ports etc)	Highly localised, concentrated cultivation of a crop or livestock
Cultivation of a crop (e.g. opium or coca) which may be targeted by bio-control techniques.	Commerical livestock systems in which animals are rapidly transported large distances, potentially leading to a quick distribution of disease.
Conflict with states suspected of biowarfare research or weapons programmes	The presence of significant "choke points" in the livestock process though which disease could be spread (e.g. centralised feed distribution points)
	Poor biosecurity surveillance and response capabilities (diagnosing an outbreak and responding effectively in order to minimise its effects)

Source: Exclusive Analysis

States with active biowarfare capabilities could easily develop anti-agricultural pathogens alongside agents harmful to humans.

Before the mid 1970s when, under the auspices of the Biological and Toxin Weapons Convention (BWC) treaty, most offensive biological weapons programmes were ended, most countries with such programmes developed anti-agricultural agents. We assess that it is likely that some states will have maintained offensive programmes, although this cannot be verified. Iraq developed wheat stem rust in the 1980s; South Africa reportedly developed its own agents, including foot and mouth disease, during the apartheid period and the US and Soviet Cold War biowarfare programmes researched the weaponisation of a variety of animal and plant pathogens. Bio-control agents have also been developed in order to target a particular crop selectively, with the United Nations Drug Control Programme, backed by the US, reportedly conducting trials in Uzbekistan in the late 1990s of Pleospora papaveracea, a fungal herbicide that targets opium poppies. State-sponsored actors would have the capability to use agricultural agents in order to undermine the economic or food stability of an adversary as a prelude to, or in conjunction with, conventional warfare. The nature of such diseases, which can occur and spread naturally (and thereby reduce the tactic's attractiveness to terrorists), offer deniability to the aggressor as it is very difficult to prove that an attack has taken place. These risks are moderated by the prohibition of such activities under the Geneva Convention and Biological Weapons Convention, and, as with other unconventional weapons, military reluctance to utilise them due to their unpredictability and particularly to the difficulties of containment to pre-defined areas.

Agroterrorism presents a number of organisational and technical challenges to terrorist groups, but requires lower capabilities than biological attacks against people.

Due to the characteristics of livestock pathogens and their ability to spread on their own, many of the problems of preparing a pathogen to make it suitable for effective dispersal as a weapon are reduced in comparison with production of pathogens aimed at humans. It is most likely that motivated and capable terrorists would succeed in producing an effective weapon for use against livestock as many animal pathogens are found widely in nature, pose little risk to individuals handling the pathogen and an infected animal or animal product can serve both as the weapon and as the vector of transmission. Nevertheless, there are technical obstacles around acquiring, storing, transporting and dispersing pathogens that terrorist groups without the existing expertise would have to overcome.

Map 1: Geographical Distribution of Naturally Occurring FMD

WAHID OIE © 2009|

Legend:
- Continuing (domestic)
- Resolved (domestic)
- Resolved (wild)
- No information

Source: World Organisation for Animal Health

Depending on a terrorist group's aims, the pathogen used and the group's ability to cultivate large numbers of infectious animals or large quantities of infected animal material and the effectiveness of biosecurity procedures, the scale of the ensuing crisis would vary considerably. Biosecurity measures that are in place to deal with naturally occurring disease in most developed countries (such as surveillance, notification and control programmes for FMD) will usually be at least partially effective against the spread of deliberately introduced pathogens, once they have been detected and identified. Table 4 illustrates hypothetical small, medium and large FMD attacks, and provides an overview of the potential consequences. The scenarios are adapted from an Australian study by an independent research commission investigating the potential impact of naturally occurring FMD on Australia. All estimates for consequences are based on the loss ratios observed in the UK 2001 FMD outbreak.

Table 4: Modelled Agroterrorism Attack Scenarios, Direct Losses ($ millions)

	Small attack	Medium attack	Large attack
Event description	Single point source FMD outbreak caused by deliberate introduction of infected livestock at central market; taking three months to stamp out and resulting in the destrution of 38,000 animals	Single point source FMD outbreak caused by deliberate introduction of infected livestock at large feedlot; taking six months to stamp out, and resulting in the destruction of 50,000 animals	Multi-source FMD outbreak caused by deliberate contamination of feedstock at multiple cattle farms; taking 12 months to stamp out and resulting in the destruction of 750,000 animals
Livestock industry export revenue losses	3,333	4,611	9,480
Livestock industry domestic revenue losses	2,373	2,944	3,332
Compensation for slaughtered livestock	4	19	41
Control costs	22	140	390
Total costs	5,732	7,714	13,243

Source: Adapted from "Impact of a Foot-and-Mouth Disease Outbreak on Australia," Productivity Commission, 2002

7. Rising Stars in al-Qaeda: The Libyan Connection

The death or capture of several senior al-Qaeda leaders since 2001, and the sidelining of Osama bin Laden as an operational force, is gradually reducing the core of older al-Qaeda veterans in top leadership positions. This extract from Exclusive Analysis' Global Jihad Analysis project profiles seven of the most prominent strategists, field commanders and spokesmen currently rising through al-Qaeda's ranks. Through evaluation of these possible next top commanders and their operational competence and objectives, we can more accurately forecast the timing, location and scale of international terrorist attacks. We also move closer to understanding whether al-Qaeda can reinvent itself as a political organisation and pose a growing global threat.

Since 2001, the death or capture of a number of senior figures associated with al-Qaeda (such as 9/11 planner Khalid Sheikh Mohammed, senior commander Abu Hamza Rabia, and Afghanistan field commander Abu Layth al-Libi) has gradually reduced the core of older al-Qaeda veterans in top leadership positions. At the same time, bin Laden appears sidelined as an operational commander, although he retains an important role as an inspirational figurehead; his communiqués are frequently out of date and in some cases contradict communiqués from other senior leaders. Meanwhile, Ayman al-Zawahiri and Mustafa Abu al-Yazid, al-Qaeda's second- and third-ranked leaders, are increasingly unrepresentative of the bulk of al-Qaeda supporters and recruits, since they represent an older generation whose formative years were spent in the Egyptian jihad.

These developments open the way for a new generation of 'rising stars' to assume positions of leadership within the organisation. It appears that al-Qaeda's old guard, led by Zawahiri, has taken the decision to bring certain younger figures to prominence, with the apparent aim of demonstrating that plenty of new leaders are waiting to replenish the ranks when older leaders are killed. While European and American recruits are helping bring al-Qaeda's message to a wider global audience, one of the most notable developments is the emergence of a Libyan cadre of jihadist veterans who are now taking on significant responsibilities as field commanders, ideologues and strategists. Formerly allied with the Libyan Islamic Fighting Group (LIFG), these Libyans fought in Afghanistan in the mid 1990s but were unable to return home due to the threat of imprisonment, and instead remained in Pakistan. There they were mentored by more senior Libyan leaders like Abu Layth al-Libi, former field commander for al-Qaeda in Afghanistan. The fact that they gained their combat experience in Afghanistan prior to 9/11 means they are long-standing and trusted allies of key al-Qaeda allies among the Afghan and Pakistan-Taliban, as well as senior al-Qaeda leaders like Zawahiri. The appearance of certain of these Libyan nationals in videos alongside Zawahiri indicates that they have been endorsed by him as worthy contenders for top leadership roles; others, like Abdullah Sa'id, have assumed military command roles, even if their media profile is low. It is likely that in the future Libyan, not Egyptian, cadres will form the core of al-Qaeda's leadership.

At present, Zawahiri himself lacks widespread popularity among jihadists. Some question his credentials; among others, he is respected, but not loved as bin Laden is. However, any transfer of power to a younger figure like Abu Yahya al-Libi, who is both able to communicate al-Qaeda's core ideas effectively, giving them contemporary relevance, and capable of strategic planning and revolutionary thought, would be likely to increase the organisation's appeal and make it a greater global terrorist threat. Any move towards far greater violence or infighting with other Islamist groups, along the lines of al-Qaeda in Iraq under Abu Musab al-Zarqawi, would be unlikely. Instead, it is likely that any strategic shift will be towards taking greater account of sympathetic Muslim public opinion and working harder to form local partnerships and alliances. While stopping short at present of involvement in political or social welfare activities along the lines of the Hizbullah or Hamas model, al-Qaeda's new generation of strategists will increasingly have to face the question of how to gain and maintain a popular mandate for peaceful rule once a territory has been seized by force. If the group succeeds in reinventing itself as a political organisation capable of ruling sections of territories like Somalia or Afghanistan, thus broadening its appeal beyond a purely extremist audience, it will become significantly more of a global strategic threat.

Exclusive Analysis tracks the evolution of this new leadership as part of our Global Jihad Analysis project through our monitoring of multilingual jihadist websites, communiqués and media releases, as well as through our expert source network and database of more than 1,000 individuals known to have been involved in jihadist terrorism, which is constantly updated with new intelligence. Below we profile seven of the most prominent strategists, field commanders and spokesmen currently rising through al-Qaeda's ranks.

Abu Yahya al-Libi

Source: http://www.adnkronos.com/AKI/English/Security/?id=1.0.2278174994

Abu Yahya al-Libi (real name Hasan Qaid, aliases Yunus al-Sahrawi and Muhammad Hasan Bakr) is a Libyan national aged around 36. Originally a member of the LIFG, al-Libi was captured in Karachi in 2002 but subsequently escaped from Bagram prison. He now plays a vital role in articulating al-Qaeda strategy, making frequent Arabic-language video appearances and authoring strategic documents. Al-Libi mostly appears on As-Sahab Media productions that are disseminated by way of al-Fajr Media. They are then posted to multiple forums, like Fallujah Forums, Ana Muslim, al-Qimmah and many others. Al-Libi has used his considerable knowledge of Islamic jurisprudence (acquired during study in Mauritania) to produce several revolutionary jihadist treatises. For example, he argues that the centuries-old scholarly prohibition on collateral damage to Muslim lives during warfare is inapplicable today, when terrorist attacks are vital to Islam's survival. He is personally ambitious and able to transmit messages that are likely to resonate with his audience. The increasing number of video appearances by al-Libi alongside prominent leadership figures suggests he is endorsed by Zawahiri and is a strong contender to take over responsibility for al-Qaeda's global strategy and operations in the event of Zawahiri's death. He is highly unlikely to be influenced by Libyan LIFG leaders' decision to renounce terrorism in 2009 (though LIFG had not successfully carried out an attack in Libya since their establishment in 1995 with the aim of toppling Libyan leader al-Gaddafi and the establishment of an Islamic state), despite the fact that his brother, a senior LIFG leader currently detained in Libya, was one of those who renounced terrorism.

Atiyah 'Abd-al-Rahman

Source: http://www.youtube.com/watch?v=t4fHIlbB0mo&feature=related

A Libyan national in his mid 30s, Atiyah 'Abd-al-Rahman (aliases Sheikh Atiyatallah and 'Abd-al-Karim al-Libi) joined al-Qaeda in Afghanistan as a teenager. Like Abu Yahya al-Libi, he later studied Islamic sciences in

Mauritania. He reportedly brokered the Algerian Salafist Group for Preaching and Combat's (GSPC) merger with al-Qaeda and he also persuaded al-Qaeda in Iraq leader Abu Mus'ab al-Zarqawi to reconcile with other insurgent groups. Zarqawi described him as 'like an older brother.' This diplomacy and awareness of the impact of negative publicity make him a valuable organisational asset. Softly spoken and scholarly, Atiyatallah made his first video appearance for al-Qaeda in spring 2009 alongside Abu Yahya. Since then he has also featured prominently alongside both Zawahiri and Abu Yahya in later releases, suggesting that Zawahiri has endorsed both men as future senior leaders and sees their roles as complementing one another, with Atiyatallah the more diplomatic and approachable character, and Abu Yahya the more driven and forceful. We think Atiyatallah is unlikely to be the same person as prolific jihadist writer Luways Atiyatallah, although even in the jihadist movement this point is debated.

Abdullah Sa`id

Source: http://www.archive.org/details/winds-of-heaven-3?start=865.5

Like Abu Yahya al-Libi, Sa'id is a Libyan national and former LIFG member. Sa'id made his first video appearance in spring 2009, in a video commemorating the life of fellow Libyan Abu Layth al-Libi, killed in a drone strike in early 2008. In February 2009, he published an article entitled 'Signs of Victory Looming in Afghanistan' in the Vanguards of Khorasan jihadist publication, which described him as the 'Head of Military Affairs in Afghanistan'. US detainee and Muslim convert Bryant Neal Vinas claims that Sa'id inherited this role from Abu Layth. Sa'id should not be confused with Mustafa Abu al-Yazid (aka

Sheikh Saeed), the overall head of al-Qaeda in Afghanistan. Abdullah Sa'id is much younger, appearing to be in his 30s. His role is probably more tactical, involving weapons training and joint military planning with the Haqqani network, for which Abu Layth was previously responsible.

Abu Talha the German

Source: http://jarretbrachman.net/?cat=7

Source: http://jarretbrachman.net/?p=13

[same person in both photos]

Abu Talha (real name Bekkay Harrach) is a 31-year-old German citizen of Moroccan origin who left Germany for Pakistan in 2007. He has appeared in several German-language videos for al-Qaeda, threatening to attack Germany if its troops do not withdraw from Afghanistan. While not a serious contender for future leadership, his value lies in his perceived ability to reach a European audience. Harrach, a former business mathematics student, has rather unusually used graphs and equations to argue for the certainty of al-Qaeda victory, whereas most al-Qaeda spokesmen rely on the Qur'an, hadith, and political or historical examples and citations to justify their views. This use of scientific empiricism, and his appearance in Western dress in a later video, was probably intended to appeal to a European audience. Der Spiegel published a report in January 2009 that quoted a local commander in Pakistan's tribal areas as saying that Harrach had received bomb-making training from senior al-Qaeda leader Abu Ubaydah al-Masri and now helps plan joint operations in Afghanistan with the Haqqani network.

Adam Gadahn

Adam Yahye Gadahn (alias Abu Azzam al-Amriki, Abu Suhayb, and Abu Suhayl) is a US citizen who has appeared in a number of English-language videos marking the anniversary of 9/11 and the London 7/7 attacks, as well as in an October 2008 video aimed at a Pakistani audience (al-Qaeda has no spokesmen fluent in Urdu). Gadahn, whose father is Jewish, converted to Islam aged 17. Moving to Pakistan, he became a translator for al-Qaeda and met senior figures Abu Zubaydah and Khalid Sheikh Mohammed. Al-Qaeda moved to boost Gadahn's credibility in June 2009, issuing his first ever video release in Arabic, in which he directly tackled criticisms of his Jewish background. Gadahn, while not a particularly effective speaker (his Arabic is read from an autocue), enjoys some popularity among English-speaking jihadists. As a non-Arab without religious schooling, he is unlikely to be a serious leadership contender, but he can nevertheless be regarded as a rising star by virtue of the fact that he is much closer to senior leaders such al-Zawahiri, who views him as a useful asset with which to communicate with and recruit from the West. The most recent videos show that al-Qaeda is trying to improve his image in the Arab world by publicly countering complaints that he is Jewish and cannot speak Arabic properly. In fact, Gadahn has attempted to turn his Jewish heritage into an asset, suggesting that he has unique cultural insights. As his Arabic improves, he is also likely to be deployed more frequently alongside other spokesmen like al-Libi.

Abu Mansur al-Shami

[no picture available – he has never appeared publicly]

Al-Shami, whose alias suggests that he is Syrian or Lebanese, has written several articles on Islamic history for the jihadist publication Vanguards of Khorasan. In August 2009, al-Shami's first audio statement was released, signalling that al-Qaeda now wishes to raise his media profile. In the statement, he cited events at the Battle of Uhud in 625 AD to argue that the death of a single leader would not prevent the jihad from continuing, stating 'The righteous only become more steadfast...when they lose their leaders', and 'One of the most serious sins that causes armies to be defeated is disobedience to the commander'. Al-Qaeda probably hopes the historical perspectives offered by al-Shami will help boost morale and prevent infighting following the loss of several senior leaders in drone strikes.

Abu Mansur al-Amriki

Source: http://www.alqimmah.net/showthread.php?p=16245

Abu Mansur al-Amriki (real name Omar Hammami) is a US citizen of Arab origin based in Somalia, who commands Arabic- and English-speaking cadres within the al-Shabab insurgent group. Hammami, aged 25, married a Somali wife in the US and was in Somalia at the time of the Ethiopian invasion in 2006. His involvement with jihadist militancy appears to date from that time. We have included Abu Mansur despite the lack of a proven operational connection to al-Qaeda, because he represents a potential conduit for the group to expand into Somalia. Abu Mansur's videos show him as an inspirational figure, able to deliver sermons and command military operations and engage with both an American and an Arab audience. He has repeatedly stated his allegiance to bin Laden, criticising other Somali groups' lack of commitment to a global jihad. We expect al-Amriki to be prominent in any future al-Qaeda franchise in Somalia.

Global Jihad and the Poetic Tradition

Poetry (or shi'r, in Arabic) is one of the oldest and most culturally significant art forms within the Arab world. Since pre-Islamic times it has performed important social functions ranging from promoting tribal cohesion, to expressing resistance to colonialism, to a rallying call for jihad. It can be difficult for external observers to understand why poetry has sometimes been taken so seriously as to prompt the censorship or imprisonment of the writer. Nevertheless, the strong tradition of Arabic social poetry and its oral performance make its audience far larger than that of poetry in the Western world, with most national newspapers featuring a poetry section.

In recognition of poetry's power for social change, Arabic jihadist forums also often include poetry sections, while al-Qaeda leaders bin Laden and Zawahiri regularly quote poetry in their speeches. Jihadist poets tend to use a formal classical style, involving traditional features like the single rhyme, to provide a poetic critique of secular rulers and Western hegemony, although the quality of the verses is often questionable. Such Such poetry echoes the paradigm of the tribal 'warrior-poet' which emerged in pre-Islamic Arabia. One example posted on the Fallujah Forums website offers a poetic defence of Salafism, a radical Islamic doctrine: 'For the land of jihad tells of its [Salafism's] manliness/ And there is nothing good about men who have forgotten their [Salafi] way.' Such high-minded sentiments are characteristic of Arabic jihadist poets, who probably see themselves as continuing a worthy tradition of classical poetry (it is notable that modernist devices like blank verse are not often used). Other poems are written in praise of particular jihadist attacks; describing the suicide attack on the USS Cole off Yemen's coast in 2000, one poet boasts 'We turned the sea to fire'.

Traditional anshidah (the plural of nasheed, or 'anthem') are also popularly used by jihadist groups as a soundtrack to their video releases. Salafis view them as the only legitimate form of song, since they are chanted by men only, without backing instruments, and focus on religious subjects. One example from an al-Qaeda in the Islamic Maghreb video posted in April 2009 and featuring testimonies of suicide bombers included the lines: 'Do not cry, Mother/ Mother, I will not return/ Mother, bid me farewell/ To the Garden of Paradise.' Despite the maudlin theme, it is performed in a rousing military style.

In contrast, jihadist poems and soundtracks in English are not hindered by any consideration of poetic heritage and convention and can hence use more contemporary and brutal language. A poem by Samina Malik, convicted in the UK in November 2007 for possession of information likely to be useful to a terrorist, contained the lyrics 'Let us make jihad/ Move to the front line/ To chop chop head of kuffar [unbelievers] swine.' Likewise, a rap soundtrack on a video released in March 2009 by the Somali al-Shabab Islamist group contained lines in English like 'Blow by blow, crime by crime, only gonna add to my avenging rhymes', aimed at a young audience more used to listening to American hip-hop. It caused controversy on jihadist forums, with some maintaining it was inappropriate for an Islamist group, while others claimed that it would help spread support for jihad internationally. Move to the front line/ To chop chop head of kuffar [unbelievers] swine.' Likewise, a rap soundtrack on a video released in March 2009 by the Somali al-Shabab Islamist group contained lines in English like 'Blow by blow, crime by crime, only gonna add to my avenging rhymes', aimed at a young audience more used to listening to American hip-hop. It caused controversy on jihadist forums, with some maintaining it was inappropriate for an Islamist group, while others claimed that it would help spread support for jihad internationally.

لنا من جندها في كلِّ يوم ٭ مصارعَ مثل ما للغابرينا

ومرّغنا كرامتها مراراً ٭ وبالمرصاد نُصليها الطعونا

ففي "الصومال" لما عاندتنا ٭ طردناها وكنا الظافرينا

وفي "الخبر" اتخذناها مجالا ٭ لتجربةٍ تُعلّم ناشئينا

وفي "كول" جعلنا البحر نارا ٭ وفي "تنزانيا" و "بأرض كينا"

وفي "منهاتن" دسنا عُلاها ٭ ودكّينا المعاقل والحصونا

وفي "الأفغان" سُمناها المآسي ٭ وأحكمنا "العراق" لها كمينا

وفي "شرق الرياض" وفي "العليا" ٭ أذقناها العذاب مكررينا

وما زلنا نقارعها سجالا ٭ نعالج حيّها حينا فحينا

وفي الأقصى لنا يومٌ قريبٌ ٭ بنصر الله حقًا واثقينا

فصرخات الأرامل واليتامى ٭ تحرّك في جوانحنا الشجونا

81

2. Africa

1. Leasing Africa – Land Rights and Investor Certainty

Sub-Saharan Africa (SSA) has nearly 25 million square kilometres of land with significant commercial agricultural potential. This article identifies the reasons why foreign agri-investment is accelerating in SSA and outlines indicators of political risk in the area of land rights. Despite ongoing government action to formalise land ownership on the basis of the Western private-ownership model, land usage rights will be a prominent issue throughout SSA for many years. The focus in this article is on agricultural investment, because of the widespread interest in food security and biofuels, but the risk indicators for land reform outlined here apply to other industries such as mining, energy and construction. Countries where investors are most likely to experience new threats to land rights are the DRC, Tanzania, Namibia, South Africa and Ethiopia.

Non-African countries are investing in Sub-Saharan Africa to improve their food security.

Poor harvests and panic buying by governments caused food prices to spike in 2008. These price moves brought food security to the policy forefront, giving precedence to concerns that rising populations and higher calorific intakes in developing countries would underpin a long-term rise in agricultural prices.

Over the last decade, SSA has become an important investment area for countries seeking greater food security. Following Saudi Arabia's announcement in January 2008 that it would phase out all domestic wheat production by 2016, Saudi agricultural companies such as Jenat have moved grain and livestock production to Egypt, Ethiopia and Sudan. The aim is to improve food security for the Gulf region, where production is declining due to the depletion of non-renewable groundwater resources.

China, in its quest for food security in the face of rising demand, is a major investor in agricultural projects in Angola, Malawi, Mozambique, Tanzania and Zambia. The first Chinese investment in African agriculture was made in a Zambian cattle ranch in 1995 by Zhongkan Farm, a private company. China's biggest agricultural interest is in Mozambique, where it is funding an agricultural research facility and has stationed over 100 agricultural experts, including some of its top rice specialists. This is in line with a 2008 promise to invest $800 million in Mozambican agriculture through Chinese state-owned enterprises, especially targeting the establishment of rice farms and cattle ranches in the Zambezi and Limpopo valleys.

African governments are welcoming agri-investment to develop rural areas, boost productivity and tax revenues and create employment.

Over the next 10 years, many African countries will offer investors incentives, such as tax breaks and free land leases, in the hope of providing employment and improving rural infrastructure. With foreign land ownership seldom possible in SSA, foreign investments are usually structured on the basis of free land leases ranging from 50 to 99 years. Deals of more than 1,000 hectares are normally negotiated between private or government-affiliated international firms and SSA government agencies.

In some instances Bilateral Investment Treaties between nations will help shape deals but typically, most will be negotiated on an ad hoc, case-by-case basis. For example, the Republic of Congo government has offered South African investors eight million hectares for maize, poultry, soya bean and dairy production, on the basis of 99-year free leases, five-year tax holidays, tax exemption on farming inputs, full repatriation of profits and the freedom to export all produce. This deal is still being negotiated. Some of the countries most actively courting agri-investors are: Angola, Botswana, Ethiopia, Ghana, Madagascar, Mali, Mozambique, Senegal, Sudan, Tanzania, Uganda and Zambia.

New capital investment and enhanced agricultural-production techniques are therefore likely to enter very underdeveloped regions. Many African governments hope that productivity improvements will spread to domestic food production, enhancing their own country's food security. Liberalisation programmes have also made many African countries eligible for development loans from multilateral lenders and from investors' home governments, enabling SSA governments to decrease their debt burdens.

Biofuels investment is particularly buoyant. Over the last five years, Brazilian, Chinese, Indian, Israeli, Western European, US and South African companies have made significant investments. These have covered traditional cash crops such as coffee, cotton and vegetables, and also expanded into sugar cane, soybeans and the jatropha plant (used for biofuel production). Ghana, Madagascar and Tanzania have hosted biofuels investments, and in 2008, the Brazilian national petroleum company, Petrobras, formed a partnership with Italian oil major, Eni, for biodiesel projects in Angola and Mozambique.

Assessing Risks to Land Investments

The following are some factors influencing the risk that disputes will arise over the land designated for a particular project:

1. National Level Factors

(i) Will governments use land as a political tool?

As two-thirds of SSA's approximately 850 million people depend on subsistence agriculture, and hence access to land, the allocation of land rights is a powerful political tool in the hands of national, regional and local governments. In Ethiopia, for example, the government is resisting the introduction of private land ownership, in part because land distribution is a convenient tool of political influence. In the early 2000s, Zimbabwe's Zanu-PF government contravened laws guaranteeing property rights and forcibly transferred white-owned land to high-ranking members of its key constituencies, such as the country's military and judiciary, to shore up support. Between 1997 and 2003, one South African commercial farmer lost Zimbabwean farms worth over $11.5 million to uncompensated expropriation.

(ii) Is land reform a stated government goal?

Some countries have long-standing and open-ended land reform policies that create high expectations among poor rural populations. Namibia and South Africa are two examples. Land reform in South Africa has followed a willing buyer/willing seller policy aimed at transferring agricultural land from a white elite to black owners. However, the political left is likely to call increasingly loudly for an acceleration of transfer during Jacob Zuma's presidency. Namibia has generally also followed a willing buyer/willing seller policy, but it has also expropriated five farms, paying appropriate compensation. Three German farmers successfully contested an expropriation in 2007.

(iii) Is a change of government likely?

Even in the absence of official policy, governments may renegotiate or revoke the deals signed by their predecessors following a change of administration. For example, in 2009 a coup in Madagascar led the incoming military government to cancel Daewoo Logistics' politically unpopular 99-year lease of 1.3 million hectares (reportedly half of Madagascar's arable land) for maize production for South Korea.

(iv) Is there a threat to the territorial integrity of the country?

For example, during 2011, contracts signed in Sudan are likely to face particular challenges as a result of the planned referendum on the independence of South Sudan. Contracts signed with either the Khartoum or Juba administrations are likely to be void depending on the outcome.

2. Local Community Benefits and Costs

Angola, Mozambique and Tanzania are particularly attractive destinations for foreign agricultural investment, as most land in these countries is legally state owned as a result of Cold War socialist experiments. This reduces the probability of successful legal challenges by third parties. However, land nominally owned by the state is in many cases actively, if unofficially, cultivated by smallholders. Deals resulting in large-scale displacement are likely therefore to encounter significant resistance. For example, in Tanzania, the government postponed all biofuels investments in October 2009 pending a clearer national policy on land procurement for biofuel production, following protests by around 5,000 rice farmers due to be evicted as part of a project.

Communal politics and land usage often make it difficult to identify parties with sufficient authority to negotiate binding and widely accepted agreements. Each case will probably present its own nuance. However, having the support of local traditional leaders, in addition to ensuring that the formal procedures are adhered to, is increasingly crucial in preventing dissent, conflict and additional demands surfacing after deals have been concluded. SSA's colonial history means that the region is particularly sensitive to perceptions of foreign exploitation. Opposition to projects is especially likely if local communities perceive foreign commercial agriculture to be a form of neo-colonialism, where foreigners use land and exploit resources without benefiting the communities.

While it may not be feasible for a company to negotiate with all potentially relevant parties, there is a risk in not involving communities in investment and land usage negotiations. Chinese investors found this to be the case when local communities protested against a cotton operation they wanted to establish on government-allocated land near Balaka in Malawi. These communities agreed, however, after Chinese projects in Zambia were presented to their leaders to demonstrate the development benefits of Chinese investment to local communities.

3. Have information systems and standards undergone reform?

In much of SSA, land-ownership frameworks have at best been modernised and formalised only over the last two decades. In most SSA countries where private land ownership is slowly being introduced, data, documents and recording systems supporting ownership claims are lacking or underdeveloped. This is particularly likely to be the case in the DRC, Mali, Uganda and Sudan. This can produce conflicting claims on land.

A recent example of this is the 2008 order by a Nigerian state court for Shell to forfeit its large Bonny Island oil terminal to local land claimants. Shell allegedly failed to obtain consent from these customary owners/occupiers of the land when it applied to the state government for ownership. Although this event was part of the ongoing enmity between certain Nigerian constituencies and Shell, it also illustrates the risk to investors of legal uncertainties surrounding land ownership in much of SSA.

4. Do water rights issues affect access or usage rights to land?

Water rights at the local level are often regulated by tradition and customary law, despite ultimate ownership usually being vested in the state. As a result, even if the state grants the investor firm water rights, there remains a risk of water-usage conflict, especially in cases where water resources are limited and subject to conflicting claims by local communities. In Kenya, for example, in May and August 2009, parliamentarians representing settlers in the Mau Forest, a key water-catchment area, defied instructions from the National Forestry Service for settlers to relocate, compromising water supplies to significant areas of the Rift Valley.

Agri-Investment in Ethiopia

In 2009, the Ethiopian government unveiled a plan to make 2.7 million hectares of prime land available to foreign (mainly Middle Eastern and Asian) investors over the next five years, with added incentives such as tax holidays and partial start-up financing from local banks. As of September 2009, it was reported that over 8,000 companies had applied for Ethiopian farmland, and that about 2,000 applications had been granted.

Ethiopia Farming Systems

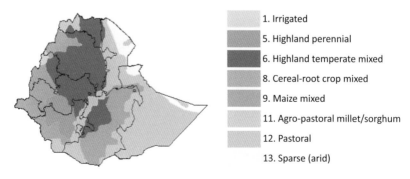

1. Irrigated
5. Highland perennial
6. Highland temperate mixed
8. Cereal-root crop mixed
9. Maize mixed
11. Agro-pastoral millet/sorghum
12. Pastoral
13. Sparse (arid)

Source: UN Food and Agricultural Office

The magnitude of this scheme has attracted criticism, especially from Western NGOs and international organisations, who claim it will drive local farmers out of business. They also argue it will not increase domestic food self-sufficiency as most food produced will be exported. However, Ethiopian civil society groups will find it very difficult to influence the state so their concerns are unlikely to have any direct impact on the actual investments other than international reputational risk for the companies involved.

The state has retained ownership of land and a strong control over agriculture, the primary export earner, and is unlikely to allow significant public protests to undermine its control over land use. India is the leading agricultural investor in Ethiopia, recording $4.3 billion as at September 2009; this is expected to reach $10 billion within the next five years. Resistance to commercial agricultural projects aimed at export is likely to be greatest in the south and east of Ethiopia, where an estimated 5.2 million people perennially require food aid.

2. Transport Development in Sub-Saharan Africa – Identifying the Big Winners

The World Bank estimates that Sub-Saharan Africa's infrastructure has improved very little over the past 30 years and in many cases has deteriorated. As a result, trade between African countries is currently less than 10% of all African gross domestic product and Africa's share of world trade is barely 2%. Africa's weak physical infrastructure has always been a major barrier to bringing its natural resources to market. This article examines some of the major infrastructure projects currently in progress and soon to be started. It highlights some of the geographies likely to see the greatest improvement and the benefits this will bring to the mining and upstream energy sectors in terms of cheaper and faster access to ports. It finishes with a focus on China's role in this development.

Multilateral Investment in African Infrastructure

Infrastructure projects linking nations together will boost regional integration and stimulate inter- and intra-regional trade.

The lack of infrastructure in southern and eastern Africa increases operating costs, forcing many firms to access world markets via South African ports. For example, mining companies in Zambia usually use Durban Port in South Africa, but with adequate infrastructure the most cost-effective routes would be through Tanzania, Namibia and Mozambique. In fact, those operating as far north as the Democratic Republic of Congo (DRC) also tend to use Durban when their nearest ports are in Angola and Tanzania.

However, Sub-Saharan African rail routes are forecast to expand by approximately 25,000km over the next 10 years, with major projects concentrated in eastern and southern Africa. Multiple-country infrastructure projects, such as the North-South Corridor and the CEMAC Trade Corridor, are set to bring significant efficiency gains to Africa's transport networks. Both of these projects are explored in more detail below.

In addition, Kenya Railways' Northern Corridor plan consists of constructing a $4 billion modern standard-gauge railway to connect Uganda and Kenya by 2011 and expanding it to the entire East African Community (EAC) by 2016. This will ease the flow of freight from Mombasa Port in Kenya to landlocked Uganda, Rwanda and Burundi. The firm is also expected to extend railway lines from Lamu to Juba and from Nairobi to Addis Ababa to enhance cargo routes towards Ethiopia and South Sudan. A transport upgrade is particularly important given projections that freight traffic at Mombassa Port will almost double to 30 million tonnes by 2030.

Another example is the planned construction of a $500 million railway line from the Moatize coal mines in Mozambique, via Malawi, to the deep-water port of Nacala by 2015. Mozambique's government intends for this to become a competitor to the congested ports of Dar es Salaam in Tanzania and Mombassa in Kenya. Brazilian mining firm Vale is expected to produce 11 million tonnes of coal a year in the Tete District of Moatize. The railway line is also expected to benefit Malawi's sugar, grain and cement trade, as well as open up new trade routes for the Zambian, Zimbabwean and Tanzanian trade of mineral resources.

The North–South Corridor will accelerate regional integration within southern and eastern Africa.

In April 2009, the World Bank, the African Development Bank, the European Union and the UK committed $1.4 billion to expand transport in eastern and

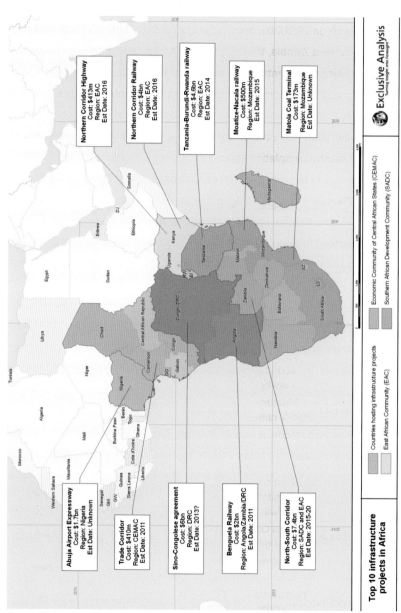

Northern Corridor Highway
Cost: $413m
Region: EAC
Est Date: 2016

Northern Corridor Railway
Cost: $4bn
Region: EAC
Est Date: 2016

Tanzania-Burundi-Rwanda railway
Cost: $4.6bn
Region: EAC
Est Date: 2014

Moatize-Nacala railway
Cost: $500m
Region: Mozambique
Est Date: 2015

Matola Coal Terminal
Cost: $173m
Region: Mozambique
Est Date: Unknown

Abuja Airport Expressway
Cost: $1.7bn
Region: Nigeria
Est Date: Unknown

Trade Corridor
Cost: $410m
Region: CEMAC
Est Date: 2011

Sino-Congolese agreement
Cost: $6bn
Region: DRC
Est Date: 2013?

Benguela Railway
Cost: $2bn
Region: Angola/Zambia/DRC
Est Date: 2011

North-South Corridor
Cost: $7.4bn
Region: SADC and EAC
Est Date: 2015-20

Top 10 infrastructure projects in Africa

Countries hosting infrastructure projects

East African Community (EAC)

Economic Community of Central African States (CEMAC)

Southern African Development Community (SADC)

Exclusive Analysis
Turning Insight into Foresight

Source: Exclusive Analysis

southern Africa. The resulting North-South Corridor project plans to construct or upgrade around 8,000km of roads and rehabilitate 600km of rail track that together connect Zambia, the DRC, Tanzania, Malawi, Zimbabwe, Botswana and South Africa. The entire plan is likely to require some $7.4 billion over 20 years to upgrade and maintain the new transport infrastructure.

The 10 most significant transport infrastructure projects in sub-Saharan Africa (ranked by completion date)

Country / Region	Project	Funding	Cost	Date of completion
Angola / Zambia / DRC	Benguela Railway	Government	$2bn	2011
CEMAC	Trade Corridor	AfDB, EU, World Bank	$410m	2011
DRC	Sino-Congolese agreement	China Exim Bank	$6bn	2013?
EAC	Tanzania - Burundi - Rwanda railway	EAC and governments	$4.6bn	2014
Mozambique	Moatize-Nacala railway	Government	$500m	2015
EAC	Northern Corridor Highway	World Bank	$413m	2016
EAC	Northern Corridor Railway	Kenya Railways	$4bn	2016
Mozambique	Matola Coal Terminal	Maputo Port Authority	$173m	Unknown
Nigeria	Abuja Airport Expressway	Federal Government	$1.7bn	Unknown
SADC and EAC	North-South Corridor	EU, World Bank, AfDB	$7.4bn	2015-20

Source: Exclusive Analysis

The project is likely to enhance intra- and inter-regional trade in Zambia and the DRC (the Copperbelt region), Tanzania, Malawi, Zimbabwe, Botswana and South Africa (gold and platinum production areas). It is highly significant for natural resources firms operating in the region because transport costs account for 20-40% of operating costs in that area (they are about 70% higher in southern Africa than they are in Europe, for example). It currently takes about two weeks to get copper from the DRC and Zambia's Copperbelt down to the coast of Tanzania or Mozambique. Mining investors in southern and East Africa are likely to face shorter delivery times and lower transportation costs to the key ports of Mombassa in Kenya and Durban in South Africa.

However, despite the initial grant of $1.4 billion in April 2009, there remain significant funding challenges for the completion of the North-South Corridor. Individual governments and donors have so far not defined their contributions to the project and financing may be slowed by the global economic downturn and lower demand for natural resources. Moreover, violent risks, particularly from rebel groups in the DRC and political violence in Zimbabwe, are also likely to obstruct the project's development. Nevertheless, the project, which may not be completed until 2015-20, has firm support from multilateral institutions such as the IMF and World Bank. Moreover, the project will probably receive support from some private investors operating in the region. Companies that are most likely to benefit from the North-South Corridor projects include: First Quantum, FreePort-McMoRan, Glencore and Vedanta, as well as Chinese operators Sicomines and NFC Africa.

Planned railway and road construction around Zambia and the DRC's Copperbelt region

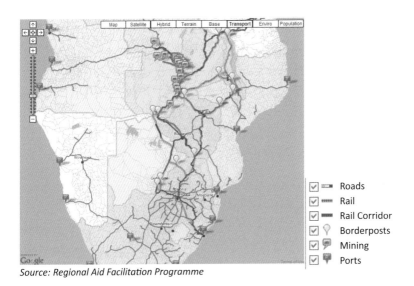

Source: *Regional Aid Facilitation Programme*

Natural resource investors in central Africa are likely to benefit from faster and cheaper access to Douala, Cameroon, with the completion of rail and road links.

The North-South Corridor's equivalent in central Africa, the Economic Community of Central African States' (CEMAC) Trade Corridor Project is financed by the African Development Bank, the European Commission, the World Bank and the French Development Agency. The project aims to improve the efficiency of trade and transport activities in central Africa, where transport costs are some of the highest in the world. Transportation costs in Chad and Cameroon, for instance, represent 52% and 33% respectively of the value of exports. Travel from either Bangui or Ndjamena to Douala, the main regional port, adds up to four weeks in additional delays due to the lack of tarred roads.

The main project of the Trade Corridor Project is the construction of the Douala-Bangui and Douala-Ndjamena roads, linking Cameroon, the Central African Republic (CAR) and Chad, as well as contributing to intra- and inter-regional trade in the CEMAC zone and improving access to world markets. Particular industries likely to benefit from the Trade Corridor will be oil services suppliers in Chad and diamond and uranium mining in the CAR. Firms such as France's Areva, De Beers, UraMin and Pangea Diamonds stand to gain from shorter and less costly delivery times. Moreover, Chad's cotton and gum exports, as well as the CAR's timber, cotton and coffee exports, are expected to benefit from improved access to Douala Port.

However, the project was initially expected to be completed by 2011 but is likely to suffer from extensive delays due to financing difficulties. Despite a $67 million transport facilitation project grant from the African Development Bank in 2007, additional funding has been slow. The project is expected to cost $410 million, although costs may overrun due to construction delays.

China's Investment in African Infrastructure

China is at the forefront of transport infrastructure development in Sub-Saharan Africa, entering deals in exchange for access to raw materials such as copper and oil.

The Export-Import Bank of China (Exim) is currently financing almost 250 infrastructure projects throughout Africa. China's state-owned enterprises, financed by Exim and other state banks, have led the way in the expansion of Africa's transport network, often as part of larger trade deals with individual countries. The China Communications Constructions Company, China's largest infrastructure development business, reported that the African market provided almost half of the company's $9.6 billion overseas revenue in 2008, with notable projects in Angola, Cameroon, the DRC, Gabon and Ethiopia.

China is responsible for between 5% and 10% of total infrastructure projects on the continent, but its role is set to increase over the next decade. During this time, China is likely to have the greatest impact on transport infrastructure development in major natural resources producers, such as the DRC and Angola (see both countries below). It may well conclude similar resources-backed loans with countries such as Zimbabwe, Niger and Ghana, to develop domestic transport infrastructures. Meanwhile, countries with few natural resources such as Malawi or Rwanda stand to benefit very little from Chinese transport infrastructure investment.

In the DRC, Chinese state-owned enterprises will invest $6 billion to improve the country's transport infrastructure, particularly the operating environment for the mining sector.

In 2007, China and the DRC government agreed to an infrastructure-for-minerals package worth $9 billion. The deal was reduced to $6 billion in August 2009 to meet IMF requirements, but is now set to go ahead; Chinese contractors have already begun several road-building projects. The package includes the development of 3,215km of railways linking the copper and cobalt mining centre in Katanga with the capital Kinshasa and the coast, as well as 6,600km of roads and highways countrywide.

The construction of all of these projects will be carried out by the China Railway Engineering Corporation and Sinohydro, with financing from China's Exim Bank. The agreement also stipulates that Congolese workers will be hired for the construction in order to boost the DRC's low levels of formal employment. In exchange, the Congolese state-owned Gecamines will cede mining rights of 10.6 million metric tonnes of copper and 620,000 tonnes of cobalt to Sicomines, a joint venture between Gecamines (32%) and a group of Chinese enterprises (68%).

Since Chinese infrastructure projects are run by Chinese firms and often bypass local bureaucracies, they are more likely to be completed on time and to be cost-effective. This $6 billion development project has no specific deadlines. However, it is likely to be completed within the next three years as Chinese investment via Sicomines is expected to begin in 2013 and this will depend on an efficient transport network. The planned construction of railways and paved roads around mining operations is particularly likely to improve the productivity and profitability of operations. A new railway line is planned between Kinshasa and Katanga, with an extension to the DRC's main port at Matadi. Although non-Chinese miners will also benefit from these projects, the development will focus primarily on Chinese mining sites.

List of transport projects under the Sino-Congolese deal (upgrading and construction)

Distance or quantity	Type of transport link	Locations
3,215km	Railways	Katanga, Bas-Congo, Kasai-Oriental, Kasai-Occidental, Bandundu, Kinshasa
3,400km	Asphalted roads	Katanga, Kisangani, South Kivu, North Kivu
135km	Restoration of roads	Matadi, Boma
135km	Restoration of roads	Mbuji-Mayi, Mwene Ditu
2,738km	Beaten earth roads	Kananga-Mbuji Mayi-Kabinda Kolwezi-Kasaji-Dilolo Dilolo-Sandoa-Kapanga-Kananga Kasaji-Sandoa Boma-Moanda-Yema NiaNia-Isiro
550km	Urban roadways	Kinshasa, Mbandaka, Bandundu, Kisangani, Kananga, Mbuji-Mayi, Lubumbashi, Matadi, Goma, Bukavu, Kindu
Two	Airport upgrades	Goma, Bukavu

Source: Information derived from the DRC Ministry of Infrastructures, Public Works and Reconstruction

Angola is undertaking a substantial overhaul of its war-ravaged transport infrastructure, funded by a $5 billion Chinese resources-backed soft loan facility.

Angola, which provides around 14% of China's oil imports, is another significant beneficiary of Chinese financing of transport infrastructure projects. One of the largest ongoing Chinese projects in Angola is the $1.1 billion construction and renovation of Lobito Port. Moreover, the rehabilitation of the Benguela Railway will open up access to Lobito Port to copper mining firms operating in Zambia's Copperbelt and the DRC, thereby significantly lowering supply times and operating costs. Investors in the Copperbelt include Camec, FreePort-McMoRan, First Quantum and Vedanta. Mining products from the DRC and Zambia are currently facing much longer transportation times and costs via Mozambique or South Africa. There is also a planned port in northern Cabinda province aimed at providing improved access to oil services providers for oil majors such as Total, BP and ExxonMobil. In Cabinda province, for example, infrastructure projects may face risk of disruption due to the ongoing offensive by the Angolan military to eradicate the remnants of the FLEC separatist rebels. Although Chinese infrastructure projects are unlikely to be directly attacked by militants, there is a small risk that the Army's heavy presence in the area will disrupt operations and increase the risk of delays and interference by the military. Frequent checkpoints manned by security forces on major roads and minor violent confrontations between the Army and the FLEC, although sporadic, are likely to increase risks to Chinese projects.

Selected transport construction or rehabilitation projects in Angola

Project	Funding	Cost	Date of completion
Barra do Dande Port	Government	Unknown	2013
Northern Cabinda Port	Government	Unknown	2013
Luanda International Airport	Government	$2bn	2011
Benguela Railway	Government	$2bn	2011
Rehabilitation of 30 local airports	Enana	$400m	Unknown
Luanda Port	Afr. Investment Bank SOGESTER	$45m $116m	2013
Viana Dry Port	Multi-Parks	$70m	2012
Catumbela Bridge, Benguela Province	Government	Unknown	2009
Benguela-Lobito road	Government	$30m	2009

Source: Information derived from Agencia Angola Press

3. Sudan: Triggers, Indicators and Realistic Scenarios for Renewed North-South War

In hotspots where a major crisis could be triggered by a relatively minor incident, our suite of risk indicators ensures our source network and intelligence collection is finely tuned to spot catalytic events and the most realistic escalation pathways. With the fifth-largest oil reserves in Africa and a significant number of humanitarian and infrastructure projects, a renewed north-South war in Sudan would have implications for commercial operators, governments and NGOs alike. Below we outline the methodological tools that enable us to identify key trigger events for a renewed civil war. With this intelligence we evaluate realistic scenarios for how a civil war would evolve and therefore some of the parameters around which intelligence-led continuity and security plans could be made. Finally, we explore potential escalation pathways involving other armed groups and states.

The 2005 Comprehensive Peace Agreement (CPA) that officially ended Sudan's north/South civil war provided for, among other things, equal sharing of oil revenues, a Government of National Unity comprising President Bashir's National Congress Party (NCP) and South Sudan's Sudan People's Liberation Movement (SPLM), demarcation of borders between north and South, nationwide elections in 2009 and a referendum on independence in South Sudan in 2011.

Implementation of these and other CPA provisions has been lacklustre. There have been disputes over border demarcation and over the results of the census that is intended to provide the basis for elections (which have therefore been postponed to 2010). The SPLM accuses the NCP of withholding its share of oil revenues and arming tribesmen in South and central Sudan in order to destabilise progress towards a referendum. In 2007, the SPLM withdrew briefly from the national government, voicing frustration with the NCP. Cooperation between the two has been symbolic since then and both sides are preparing for war. Both the elections in 2010 and the referendum in 2011 are particular flashpoints.

Balance of Forces

Our sources in Sudan confirm that both sides have been re-arming significantly over the last two years, most likely in preparation for renewed conflict. The Southern People's Liberation Army (SPLA), which numbers around 20,000-30,000 strong, has been increasing its capabilities to help redress the balance with the much better-equipped northern Sudan Armed Forces (SAF), which have over 100,000 active members, including 105,000 Army troops, 1,300 naval forces, a 3,000-strong Air Force and 17,500 paramilitary forces. For example, in late 2007, the SPLA took delivery of 30+ Ukrainian T-72 tanks, and in June 2008 the South Sudanese Parliament authorised the creation of air and riverine units to enhance the SPLA's capability. According to our sources, the SPLA has taken delivery of upwards of 100 tanks since 2007, most of which were shipped from Ukraine to Kenya, but possibly also from Ethiopia; in July 2008, the UN observed 18 T-55s entering Blue Nile State from across the Ethiopian border, although there has been some dispute over whether these were new tanks or tanks that had been in Ethiopia for repairs.

The SPLA's aim is to counter the SAF's air superiority and provide security along the White Nile, which runs from the north through to the South's capital, Juba, and on to Uganda. Talks are under way on the riverine unit and it is likely that external defence contractors will be involved in supplying and maintaining the boats, as well as providing training. A general has been appointed to head the air wing, but there is currently little equipment or trained capacity and anti-air installations are mostly ad hoc at various bases and airports. The SPLA has also been receiving training from the Kenyan Army, mostly for SPLA non-commissioned officers. Our sources report some of this is also likely to include training to use the Ukrainian T-72 tanks, which Kenya denies, and other weaponry (such as BM-21 multiple rocket launchers, RPG-7V anti-tank weapons, and anti-aircraft guns) it has been importing via Kenya since 2006. For its part, the SAF, which has around 63 combat-capable aircraft, including scores of fighter jets and attack helicopters, has increased weapons purchases from China and is stockpiling ammunition. Recent purchases from China include Type-92 wheeled infantry-fighting vehicles that have been upgraded with 2A72 30mm guns. Other Chinese hardware includes new generation Type-96 and Type-85-II, and upgraded Type-59D main battle tanks. Northern Sudan has at least five main military factories capable of producing ammunition as well as tanks, armoured vehicles, assault rifles, rocket-propelled grenades, mortars, military electronics and aviation equipment. Unconfirmed reports from our sources indicate that the SPLA claim to have the capability to assemble military aircraft and produce vehicles.

However, although this indicates increased preparedness for war, the relative balance of military power is unlikely to affect the duration of renewed conflict, as the last civil war showed. Despite the north's advantage in terms of equipment (particularly SAF air supremacy), a quick win is far from guaranteed. Although both sides are building capability for a conventional land war, in reality the war is most likely to involve much smaller confrontations, the use of proxies and guerrilla tactics. Nonetheless, the weaponry amassed by the two sides is likely to be deployed, and aerial capability in particular is likely to lead to notable property destruction and loss of life in urban centres in the South.

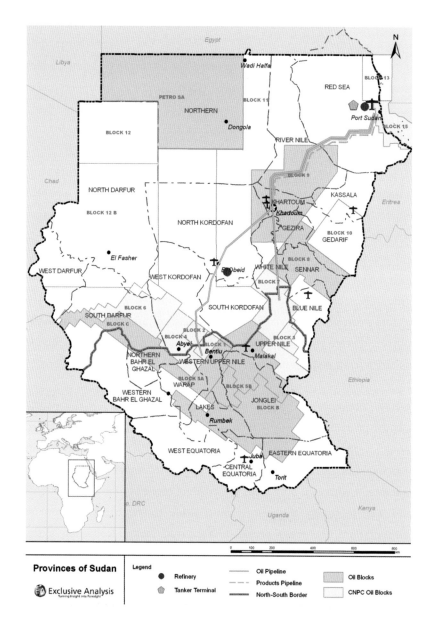

106

Triggers for Civil War

For South Sudan, war would jeopardise the progress made in infrastructure development since the end of the last civil war, and for President Bashir in northern Sudan there would be the risk of provoking a wider conflict involving Darfuri rebels and his enemy to the west, Chad. Nevertheless, the longer the provisions of the CPA continue unimplemented, the more likely there is to be a local incident, with key flashpoints being transition areas in the central belt like Abyei, Blue Nile and South Kordofan/Nuba Mountains, that will spiral into a wider civil war. Also, the probability of either side deliberately starting a war would increase if they believed the CPA to be irretrievably broken.

The most likely developments that would lead to renewed fighting include those we list below. Alongside each trigger we have included some of the key risk indicators - developments that suggest each particular trigger was becoming more likely. There is evidence that some of the developments listed are already happening.

• **The SPLM pulls out of the unity government again, citing the NCP's failure to implement the CPA.** Indicators: **(1)** increased SPLM complaints about the census; **(2)** NCP victory in national elections; **(3)** halted delivery of the South's share of oil revenue; **(4)** SPLM blame NCP for interfering with the Permanent Court of Arbitration's ruling on the border dispute around Abyei; **(5)** evidence of support from NCP of proxy militias or the Lord's Resistance Army (which it used as a proxy in the last civil war).

• **The SPLM splits formally as a result of a power struggle between those supporting a unified Sudan in which Southern rights are protected (the late SPLM leader John Garang's 'New Sudan' policy) and those insisting on a**

'South first' policy, i.e. unilateral declaration of independence. SPLM leader Salva Kiir, himself an ardent secessionist, will have trouble balancing the two camps. Indicators: **(1)** public quarrels between key representatives of the New Sudanists (northerners based around SPLM Secretary General Pagan Amum) and those from the South-first camp (based around Salva Kiir); **(2)** Salva Kiir agrees to boundaries in the transitional areas that are seen as a concession to NCP demands; **(3)** one of the late SPLM leader John Garang's close allies bids for leadership of the party ahead of elections.

• **President Bashir is replaced by a hardliner (for instance, as a result of being arrested to face war-crimes charges in The Hague, dying in office or being removed from the leadership of the NCP).** Indicators: **(1)** hardliners within Bashir's NCP push for more action to prevent Southern cessation, creating fractures in the party; **(2)** Bashir sides with other NCP members against the party elite, who hail mostly from the Shaigiya, Danagla and Jaaliya tribes from areas around the Nile north of Khartoum; **(3)** Bashir publicly falls out with the influential Salah Gosh, whom he moved from his long-term post of intelligence chief to become presidential adviser in August 2009; **(4)** Sudan's Second Vice President Osman Taha joins forces with Bashir opponent Hassan al-Turabi, significantly increasing their joint control over the NCP.

• **The NCP ignores South Sudanese reservations about the population census and pushes ahead with elections in 2010.** Indicators: **(1)** elections are called, despite SPLM objections about the process; **(2)** the NCP unilaterally passes election laws, deciding on district/boundaries regardless of SPLM agreement; **(3)** Bashir launches an election campaign.

• **The SPLM, which has been making inroads into the NCP's northern support base and aligning with Darfuri groups, wins the national election.** Indicators: **(1)** northern parties, including Umma, Democratic Union Party and Hassan al-Turabi's Popular Congress Party, endorse the SPLM; **(2)** the SPLA nominates someone with a large following among Kordofanis, Darfuris and Beja for a top position in a post-election administration, such as Abdel Aziz Adam al-Hillu; **(3)** the SPLA formally announces a coalition with other parties that have broad support bases in disputed areas.

• **South Sudanese vote for independence in the 2011 referendum.** Indicators: **(1)** SPLM and pro-secession politicians do well in national elections; **(2)** New Sudanists in the SPLA endorse secession. NOTE: In August 2009, the US-based National Democratic Institute (NDI) presented the Governors' Forum in South Sudan's Parliament with poll results showing over 90% support.

Scenarios for a Return to Civil War

The most likely outcome is a return to protracted civil war, which would not necessarily be preceded by a formal declaration of war, in which neither side is capable of achieving a decisive victory. Kordofan and its oilfields are certainly a key flashpoint for direct encounters between the SAF and SPLA. The SAF would seek to engage the SPLA in the South as well, with airstrikes on Juba and the use of proxy militias (Nuer and Murle tribesmen and LRA rebels) elsewhere in the South. Here we consider how a return to civil war might evolve and which areas would be most affected. We then analyse some possible escalation pathways beyond a north-South civil war, including attacks by Darfuri groups on Khartoum, inter-state war between Chad and Sudan, a wave of attacks on northern Sudan by jihadist groups and the intervention of an international coalition.

Initial Conflict Scenarios

Civil War Scenario 1: Large-scale sustained fighting between the SAF and SPLA along the border in Kordofan and central areas, with northern airstrikes on Southern cities, including Juba.

Probability: This is the most likely development pathway for a return to civil war; both sides are preparing for this possibility and seeking alliances with the Misseriya, Dinka and other tribal militias in these areas to boost their standing armies.

Description: Fighting in central areas such as Southern Kordofan/Nuba Mountains, Unity State, Abyei and Jonglei is likely in any war scenario, as this is where the disputed border and the bulk of the country's oil wealth is located. A formal unilateral declaration of independence by South Sudan would almost certainly be preceded by the military warning indicator of a build up of its infantry and armour in defensive positions along the border in Kordofan. If the AU, US, EU and Arab efforts to broker talks between the SPLM and NCP failed following a unilateral declaration of independence, which is likely, heavy fighting would almost certainly erupt between the northern-controlled Sudan Armed Forces (SAF) and the South Sudan People's Liberation Army (SPLA). There are already many SAF and NCP infiltrators in the Southern communities that could be used to propagate proxy war first; after a few weeks, northern forces could then claim to be moving in to provide security the SPLM cannot deliver. Northern forces would have air supremacy, which it is very likely they would use to launch airstrikes on infrastructure, military and SPLM assets in Juba. While this would cause significant property damage, it would not be sufficient to disable the SPLA and their allies.

Commercial implications: Energy operations in the Heglig, Bamboo, Defra and Unity oilfields around Kordofan would be at particular risk. As the fields are likely to be heavily contested, abandoned drilling equipment and infrastructure would be significantly damaged. Sudan's two major pipelines – Petrodar (running from Palogue to Port Sudan) and the Greater Nile Oil Pipeline (running from the Heglig and Unity fields to Port Sudan) – both cross the north-South border and would risk being damaged. The northern Air Force would probably target roads and bridges out of the South's capital, Juba, to disrupt SPLA supply lines. This would lead to numerous **civilian casualties** as well as disruption to the **delivery of aid** in the South.

Civil War Scenario 2: Widespread low-level violence in South Sudan, initiated by tribal militias sponsored by the NCP. The SPLA retaliates by launching attacks on the bases of northern troops along the north-South border.

Probability: Fighting between tribal militias has already been increasing in South Sudan, some of it very likely sponsored by the NCP. However, this would almost certainly escalate significantly if the SPLM were to win 2010 elections or 2011 referendum results were pro-independence. The NCP is already supporting several groups both financially and with arms supplies to ensure they can be used as proxies against the SPLA.

Description: LA units and tribes allied to the SPLA, like the Dinka, are most likely to be confronted by Nuer and Murle tribal militia around the Sabot and White Nile rivers and around Malakal and Akobo in **Jonglei** and **southern Upper Nile states**. The Murle would probably also launch attacks on SPLA units in **Juba** in an effort to tie the SPLA down in its defence, although it is unlikely to take the city. Uganda's rebel Lord's Resistance Army (LRA) would be encouraged by the NCP to move from current locations in the tri-border area of DRC, Central African Republic and Sudan to attack deeper into southwestern Sudan – **Western and Central Equatoria**. The SPLA itself would also be likely to retaliate directly against northern troops, particularly in Damazine **(Blue Nile State)** with SPLA forces in the state, in Kaduglie **(South Kordofan)** with Division 9 from South Kordofan, positions north of Abyei with forces stationed just south of the disputed town and SAF positions at oilfields using SPLA divisions 4 and 5.

Commercial Implications: NGOs, energy and **construction** assets around Juba and elsewhere in the South (especially Jonglei, Upper Nile, Western and Central Equatoria) will be at risk of attacks from proxy militia aligned to President Bashir's government. The SPLA security response, which would include arming its own allies, and **cargo** transport by road, will also be at risk of attacks from pro-NCP militia. Risks to road shipments would be highest along the Uganda-Yei-Juba, Kenya-Kapoeta-Torit-Juba and Malakal-Melut/Adar routes. In this scenario, risks in Khartoum would be significantly lower than in Southern and central areas, although this would change if Escalation Scenario 3 were triggered.

Widening Conflict: Escalation Pathways

Escalation Scenario 1: Darfuri rebels use the renewed fighting in the South to attack Khartoum, forcing the SAF to fight on two fronts.

Probability: Darfuri rebel groups are currently engaged in talks with the government, but Khalil Ibrahim's Justice and Equality Movement (JEM) and Abdul Wahlid Al-Nur's Sudan Liberation Movement (SLM) do not have any faith in President Bashir's willingness to compromise. In the event of open hostilities between the north and South, the JEM in particular would be very likely to attempt an attack on Khartoum, if only to ensure a seat at the table at any future peace negotiations – the 2005 Comprehensive Peace Agreement between north and South excluded Darfuri groups.

Description: A JEM attack on **Khartoum** would probably start with Khartoum Airport and Omdurman. This is likely to be supported by the SPLA, with a number of battle wagons (civilian vehicles modified to carry large-calibre automatic weapons), who would attempt to force the SAF to deploy more troops to protect the city. In response, the NCP would order areas of the city populated by several thousand Darfuris and South Sudanese to be cordoned off, most likely by the semi-paramilitary People's Defence Force (PDF). Government opponents in the city would be rounded up. President Bashir would almost certainly accuse Western countries of supporting South Sudan and limit movements of Western expatriates in the city and in and out of the north of the country. A JEM attack on Khartoum is very unlikely to last longer than a few days, and it is very unlikely it will be able to take the city or the airport, given the SAF's military supremacy. The aim would be to embarrass the government, sow suspicion towards senior intelligence and military officials and damage the confidence of the northern population. Road blocks and enhanced security would be likely to last over a month.

Commercial implications: A heavy battle for the **airport** would result in damage to its infrastructure and aircraft on the ground. Commercial flights would be suspended. Fighting between Darfuris, Southerners and the PDF would cause **property** damage in the city, most extensively in Omdurman where Western assets are limited. However, **Westerners** and their **embassies** and foreign **NGO** offices and staff would be at significant risk of attack by the PDF and would almost certainly have their movements restricted; this would apply particularly to the residential neighbourhoods close to the airport like Amarat and Khartoum 2.

Map of Khartoum

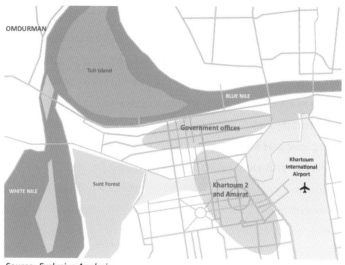

Source: Exclusive Analysis

Escalation Scenario 2: Chad moves forces across the border, forcing the SAF to fight both a civil war and an inter-state conflict.

Probability: This scenario could occur independently but could also follow on from Civil War Scenario one or two or Escalation Scenario one. Chad's President Deby is very keen to see Bashir deposed and is also likely to see renewed north-South fighting as an opportunity to score success against Chadian rebels based in Darfur.

Description: Chadian forces would be likely to use the opportunity to target Chadian rebel bases inside Sudan with airstrikes and cross-border infantry and artillery attacks. Chad would also hope to help remove Bashir from power, although this is unlikely to happen. This is likely to involve Chadian troop movement across the border into Darfur from eastern Chad. Chad's capabilities include one armoured battalion, seven infantry battalions, one artillery battalion, four combat-capable aircraft and attack helicopters. Movement would be supported by the Chadian Air Force, which would bomb SAF positions in western Sudan. This would force Sudan to divert some aircraft to defend against the air attacks and launch counterattacks inside Chad, most likely on the capital, N'Djamena. France would almost certainly provide intelligence from French reconnaissance aircraft based in Chad and ammunition via Libya to support Deby. UNAMID peacekeepers in Darfur would come under pressure to intervene, but Security Council authorisation would be unlikely as it would probably be blocked by France. Instead they would have to focus on protecting refugees in Darfur while under attack from pro-northern militia.

Commercial Implications: The Chadian Air Force would strike **military**, **government** and **commercial** targets around Khartoum and Darfur. Preferred targets in Khartoum would be government buildings and security forces assets, although anti-air defences towards Khartoum would probably force Chad to limit its actions to Darfur. **Aid operations** around Abeche in eastern Chad and El Fasher and El Geneina in Darfur would be severely disrupted. In Darfur, militia on both sides would almost certainly raid **NGO** operations for supplies and aid flows would be severely disrupted.

Escalation Scenario 3: An international coalition intervenes militarily to restore the status quo and the integrity of the north-South border.

Probability: Bashir's government is extremely unlikely to allow this to happen. If it were to be allowed, it is likely to be because Bashir calculated that the presence of a peacekeeping force in contested oil-rich areas would allow energy operations, and the revenue they bring, to continue. Western nations are likely to be unwilling to contribute troops. Intervention is therefore most likely to be limited to redeploying UNAMID peacekeeping troops already based in Darfur. However, if Bashir's government was overthrown by other northerners objecting to Bashir's policy vis-à-vis the South the likelihood of peacekeepers being accepted would increase.

Description: Following months of heavy fighting around oilfields, the AU, with UN backing, is mandated to deploy troops in a 'buffer zone' along the north-South border to keep the two sides apart while talks continue. The AU would deploy no more than 2,000 troops to the zone as they are already stretched with troop commitments in Somalia and member-state participation in UN missions elsewhere. Peacekeepers have a peacekeeping mandate only and are not able to secure the zone effectively as they cannot actively engage either northern or Southern troops or their proxies. Therefore attacks by the SPLA and their proxies would continue, specifically targeting northern troops but also energy installations in order to disrupt oil revenue for the north.

Commercial Implications: The deployment would allow oil operations in contested areas like Abyei to continue, which in turn would help fund Bashir's war effort. If a share of these funds is not returned to South Sudan (as is very likely to be the case) the SPLA and its proxies would be likely to intensify attacks intended to disrupt energy operations, in the process bringing them into confrontation with peacekeepers. The areas in question have oil blocks currently operated by consortiums that include China National Petroleum, Petronas, ONGC Videsh and Sudapet. These would almost certainly suffer from some disruption to production even though it is unlikely operations would be completely closed down.

Escalation Scenario 4: Islamist militants stage attacks on Western targets in the capital, Khartoum, and other parts of East Africa.

Probability: The likelihood of jihadist attacks in Khartoum would be enhanced by any overt Western and East African support for South Sudan. They would be most likely if South Sudan were to secede unilaterally, with backing from the US, Kenya, Uganda and France (which would be more likely to support secession if Total were allowed to keep oil block 5), or if there were a military intervention in support of the South. Having hosted Osama bin Laden in 1992-96 and been the target of a US bombing of a pharmaceutical company in 1998 (in retaliation for bombings of US embassies in East Africa), Sudan is very likely to be embraced as a cause by the global jihad movement if the West was seen to intervene against the Khartoum government.

Description: Home-grown Islamist militants would target assets associated with countries perceived to be wrongfully supporting the South and attempting to overthrow the Islamist north. If there were a military intervention, there would almost certainly be calls from leaders within the global jihad network – like Ayman al-Zawahiri – to support the Sudanese north and to travel to Sudan to wage jihad against external states with a presence in the country.

Already-active militant groups, mainly in Khartoum, would target Western assets in the capital with suicide bombs, including truck bombs. The northern government would choose to turn a blind eye to their planning, unlike previous security operations against Islamic militants. An explosion at a house in the Al Salama district, a poor residential area in Khartoum, on 12 August 2007, was blamed by the government on a militant Islamist group based in Khartoum and led to around 150 arrests across the city. This was followed in September 2007 by door-to-door weapons searches by security forces in Al Salama. Although the Sudanese security services exert significant control in Khartoum, they include factions that overtly encourage militant Islamic views. This, alongside an imperative for the government to turn a blind eye to jihadist activity that targets its opponents, opens up an operating space for foreign and local jihadists in and around the capital.

Commercial Implications: This would specifically increase terrorism risks to international embassies, expatriates and NGOs in Sudan, as well as Kenya, Ethiopia and Uganda. The Somali/Ogaden network could be used to operate in Ethiopia and Kenya in particular. In Sudan, bombing risks would be greatest in Khartoum where embassies are located, but Western NGOs – especially those operating in Darfur or central areas like Kordofan/Blue Nile, Jonglei and Unity State – would face significantly increased kidnap risks. The main commercial airports in north and South Sudan would also be attractive targets as they are used by large numbers of Westerners. The security at both airports is very poor and Juba International Airport lacks basic security measures, such as metal detectors.

3. Asia

1. Afghanistan: 360° Strategic Risk Review

While Afghanistan continues to challenge Western policymakers, new commercial opportunities are emerging in the natural resources sector alongside an ongoing need for aid work and cargo movement. Through detailed understanding of the regional and group dynamics along with an assessment of the International Security Assistance Force's (ISAF) proposed military strategy with potential implications for troop deployment, we forecast key security risks to civilian and military operators in the one-year outlook. The following includes analysis of risks of kidnapping and attacks on hotels, as well as risks to cargo, aviation, aid workers and energy assets. We also consider the effectiveness of counter-insurgency operations as the insurgency grows increasingly fractured and examine the effect of an improved operating environment in FATA, Pakistan, on the ability of militants to undertake more ambitious attacks inside Afghanistan.

General McChrystal's proposed strategy is unlikely to be sufficiently resourced to a level that will allow improvement in the situation in Afghanistan in the coming five years.

General McChrystal, the commander of the ISAF in Afghanistan, has submitted a proposal for 10,000-50,000 more troops to President Obama to support his renewed counterterrorism strategy. The additional troops are seen as vital in order to regain the initiative from the Taliban and adopt a strategy that will be more focused on protecting the Afghan civilian population, with emphasis being placed on securing population centres and accelerating the growth of Afghan security forces' capabilities. As McChrystal's proposal faces competition from counterterrorism strategies, such as the one advanced by US Vice President Joe Biden, it is unlikely to be fully implemented but rather combined with Biden's proposal.

However, even if Obama decides to implement McChrystal's proposal, evidence of fraud in the elections has discredited the very government that NATO troops are there to support and has entrenched President Karzai's supporters. This will make it harder to appeal to reconcilable Afghans who might have agreed to turn against the Taliban, since now they would be allying themselves with a discredited President Karzai. In addition, troop shortages, and constraints that some troop and training providing nations have applied to their contingents, further limit capability. In turn, it is therefore unlikely that Afghan Army and police training targets can be fully met, especially not the enhanced targets proposed by McChrystal. The Afghan population will more logically hedge their loyalties since the entire exercise is geared towards an exit strategy.

In the absence of an Afghan government that commands consensus, and the lack of an overarching integrated civil-military campaign plan, we (and many others) assess that General McChrystal's recommended military strategy is thus unlikely to achieve sustainable progress in the timeframe that US and NATO politicians will need to satisfy their electorates. Even if resourced and implemented, his recommendations will not overcome the lack of unity of civil/military effort, the lack of NATO national governments' buy-in to a master strategy or the deficiencies in the Afghan government.

We therefore foresee an exit in the three- to five-year outlook with a drawdown starting in 2011. The intelligence for a direct causal relationship between operations in Afghanistan and the prevention of attacks on Western soil is presently absent, which will undermine the political case for longer-term presence. In fact, those Western fighters who do make it to Afghanistan engage there and are not presently returning with enhanced skills, knowledge or resources in the way that foreign fighters were pre-2001. Further, given that the US and NATO have been unable to stop militants crossing the border into neighbouring Pakistan's tribal areas and that militant groups in the tribal areas are increasingly likely to cooperate with each other, we assess that the ability of foreign jihadists to attack the West has increased (see the article Pakistan in 2010: New Alliances, New Risks?). The case for concentrating resources in Afghanistan will be further politically weakened if there is another attack on Western targets traced to a country other than Afghanistan, such as Somalia, Sudan or Yemen. In short, there are probably faster ways to deliver national security objectives that bypass the provision of social services and infrastructure in Afghanistan.

A compliant Afghan strongman, or more likely a series of local compliant strongmen, is a highly plausible scenario that would enable an ISAF exit while preserving Western national security objectives. We are also watching closely for signs of increased Chinese involvement. We already see some and consider a large-scale Chinese commercial intervention in the three- to five-year outlook a relevant and moderately likely scenario. Although less likely than a commercial expansion, there are presently weak indicators that suggest it would be militarily supported. The plausibility of this scenario arises from a revised Chinese military exercise pattern to reflect land-based peace support operation scenarios, their shared concern for al-Qaeda in the region, a close relationship with Pakistan and their successful $3.5 billion bid for the Aynak copper mine, south of Kabul.

The insurgency is likely to grow increasingly fractured, with the eastern and southern insurgencies becoming more distinct in terms of tactics, leadership and ideology. This is likely to make counter-insurgency and dialogue efforts less effective in the coming year.

We expect violence to rise most dramatically in the east and the south of Afghanistan as militants fight to defend themselves against increased numbers of US troops deployed in the first half of 2009, especially in Kandahar, Helmand, Wardak, Logar and Kunar. While coalition troops have succeeded in establishing safe zones in the south and the east, militants' operational capabilities are unlikely to be significantly reduced. Increasing distinctions in tactics, leadership and ideology between the eastern and southern insurgencies are likely to make counter-insurgency and dialogue efforts less effective. The drug-funded independence of local Taliban commanders, especially in the south, means that any counter-insurgency gains made in the east will be less relevant in the south and vice versa. Despite the increased US/NATO effort being applied to recruiting and training the much-expanded Afghan security forces, the transfer of prime responsibility for security to the Afghan government is unlikely to be fully achieved by McChrystal's 2010 target or the initial 2011 target.

Risks rated map, Afghanistan by province

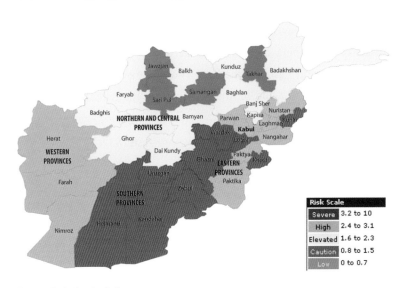

Source: Exclusive Analysis

Cooperation between militant groups in Pakistan's FATA is likely to improve, heightening the risk of both cross-border attacks into Afghanistan and more ambitious attacks overseas.

In the coming year, we judge that Pakistan's Federally Administered Tribal Areas (FATA) are likely to provide a more effective safe haven for jihadist groups than Afghanistan. There have been a number of successful US drone attacks against 'high-value targets' such as Baitullah Mehsud, Abu Khabab al-Masri and Usama al-Kini, which have led to some fragmentation of command and succession disputes, for instance within the Tehreek-e-Taliban Pakistan (TTP). However, other factors work in favour of jihadists in those areas of the FATA and neighbouring Malakand area that are not subject to US surveillance. The main reason is that external pressure from both US and Pakistan forces has made Pashtuns concentrate on confronting external attacks, diminishing local inter-group feuds. These feuds very often centred on foreigners being hosted by a rival and therefore created difficulties for non-Pashtun jihadists. There is evidence that previously disparate militant groups in the FATA are uniting in the face of US interference and by extension are more willing to enhance their cooperation with Kashmiri and Punjabi groups.

In Kabul, attacks targeting security forces, government and diplomatic assets in the Wazir Akbar Khan, Shash Darak, Centre, Shar-e-Now and Taimani areas are likely to increase, as are kidnappings and hotel attacks. More attacks in Kabul are likely in the coming year as militants seek to mount attacks on high-profile targets to challenge the government's ability to maintain security, even in the capital. In 2008, there were about 30 attacks in Kabul, with nearly half of them occurring in the last three months of the year. As of 20 August 2009 there had already been at least 32 attacks in Kabul.

The use of asymmetric tactics, such as suicide, roadside and car bombings and indirect fire of rockets and mortars, is likely to increase. Successful vehicle bomb attacks have already been carried out against ISAF headquarters on 15 August 2009 and Kabul International Airport on 8 September 2009. While neither installation was penetrated or seriously damaged, headlines were made and casualties inflicted on NATO forces in supposedly secure areas. Both the technical sophistication and the tactical employment of improvised explosive devices are likely to improve and increase security force casualties, including among those NATO troop contributors whose commitment to the campaign is already under strain. There is also an increased probability of coordinated attacks involving multiple targets. The 10 February 2009 simultaneous attack on the ministries of justice and education and the prison directorate demonstrated that insurgents have both the intent and capability to launch such operations. Similar attacks have since been staged in Khost and Gardez (Paktia). Attacks on multiple targets, especially those involving suicide and truck bombs, are likely to be the preferred tactic in Kabul in the next year. The majority of attacks will target security forces, government and diplomatic assets in the Wazir Akbar Khan, Shash Darak, Centre, Shar-e-Now and Taimani areas, where most of these assets are located. A wider range of government ministries are likely to fall within the militant target set in the coming year, including the Ministry for Tribal and Border Affairs.

Kidnapping rings controlled by criminal gangs in Kabul have grown in strength, especially in the Karte Parwan district where many of them are based. Cooperation between local police and kidnapping rings has grown, increasing kidnapping for ransom risks for foreigners and rich Afghans in the one-year outlook. We also expect militants to undertake assassination and kidnapping attempts against government, diplomatic and military figures, including ministers and Western ambassadors. Additionally, expatriates are at risk of attack in hotels, guesthouses and restaurants catering to foreign residents, especially in the Wazir Akbar Khan district. L'Atmosphere, The Gandamak Lodge, Taverna du Liban and other hotels/restaurants have employed private security firms to provide guards but are still vulnerable to attack. Despite increases in security, militants are likely to attempt suicide attacks against major hotels, including the Serena and the Safi Landmark Hotel.

Risks of attack on overland cargo are most likely to increase in and around Kabul and on the southern portion of the Ring Road as militants intensify their efforts to disrupt US/NATO supplies.

In the one-year outlook, militants operating in Kabul and neighbouring provinces, particularly Wardak and Ghazni, are likely to stage more attacks on US/NATO cargo supplies bound for troops in the south. Risks of attack on cargo convoys, particularly in the form of roadside bombs and ambushes, are likely to increase on routes in and out of Kandahar, namely on the Kandahar and Helmand stretches of the Ring Road, especially in Panjwayi and Maiwand districts. Routes to/from Lashkar Gah (in Helmand) also face rising risks of attack given the probable increase in US/NATO supplies arriving via the airport, as do the airport roads in Kandahar and Kabul.

Risks to overland cargo moving between Pakistan and Afghanistan are substantial, especially on the Khyber Pass on the Peshawar-Jalalabad-Kabul road, where attacks are likely to occur frequently in the coming year. In February 2009, militants destroyed a bridge on the pass, disrupting cargo for many days. Attacks are less frequent at the Chaman border crossing, but cargo is also at risk. In June 2009, militants attacked a NATO supply terminal there and destroyed four trailers. Despite the opening of new routes for non-lethal supplies through Uzbekistan and Tajikistan (known as the Northern Distribution Network), US/NATO forces remain reliant on the Khyber Pass route, which transports roughly 70% of their overland cargo.

Cargo entering Afghanistan from new northern routes will face lower risks of attack than on routes through Pakistan, but risks of attack will increase near Kabul.

The US is currently working to expand the use of two northern overland cargo routes that pass through Russia and Kazakhstan and then through Tajikistan or Uzbekistan into Afghanistan. The routes opened with the first shipment of non-lethal goods in February 2009. In June and July 2009, a daily average of only seven NATO cargo containers entered Afghanistan from these routes, far below the planned 200 per day, due to physical and political bottlenecks. From the northern borders, the routes go through the Salang tunnel and connect to Afghanistan's Ring Road, which connects to Kabul and Kandahar. NATO cargo routes from the north will almost certainly attract militant attacks, although cargo on any of these routes will face lower risks of attack than on the routes through Pakistan. Risks of attack are lowest in Uzbekistan, as Islamist groups there, including the Islamic Movement for Uzbekistan, have lower capabilities than local insurgent groups in Tajikistan. Cargo is more likely to be targeted by militants near Kabul than in the north.

While the amount of cargo shipped via the Uzbekistan and Tajikistan routes is likely to increase over the next year, the US will nonetheless face logistical challenges due to its need to supply the enhanced troop deployments of early to mid 2009, move lethal cargo and manage long supply chains that cross through several countries. Russia's opposition to increased US military influence in the region and the fact that the northern routes can only be used for non-lethal cargo mean that NATO will continue to rely on routes through Pakistan.

Increased use of air transport for US/NATO cargo is likely to lead to more militant attempts to target aviation assets in the coming year.

For security reasons, NATO has reduced the amount of military cargo passing through Pakistan and is increasing its cargo flights (mostly into Kabul and Kandahar airports). In July 2009, Kyrgyzstan agreed to allow the US to continue transporting some 500 tonnes of supplies per month to Afghanistan from Manas Airbase. Fuel and oil supplies as well as heavy vehicles and non-lethal equipment will continue to be transported overland, but personnel, their equipment, ammunition and rations can be transported by air. As militants are likely to focus attacks on US/NATO cargo in the one-year outlook to disrupt supplies to larger US troop deployments in the south, attempts to attack US/NATO aviation assets are likely to increase. Insurgent attacks will be primarily directed against military and private contractor helicopters, and to a lesser extent airports used by military forces, with far fewer attacks on commercial aircraft.

Risks are most significant while aircraft are on the ground, in the form of rockets and mortars fired into airports and suicide bombings on airport perimeters, rather than aircraft being shot down.

Security measures at Bagram Airbase and Kabul International and Kandahar airports reduce risks of attack within the premises, but militants are likely to attempt suicide bombings near security posts as well as rocket and mortar attacks, resulting in some limited property damage. A vehicle bomb attack at the entrance to Kabul International Airport occurred on 8 September 2009, killing three; a similar attack occurred at Bagram Airbase in March 2009, injuring three US contractors. Lashkar Gah Airport, where aircraft are frequently attacked by small arms fire, is particularly at risk. There was a roughly 65% increase in surface-to-air attacks in 2008, primarily in the form of rocket-propelled grenades (RPGs), the overall number of aircraft of all types shot down in 2008 was roughly 10, including at least three coalition helicopters. In 2009, as of October, four coalition helicopters have been destroyed as a result of hostile fire.

Violent risks to airports, Afghanistan

Airport	Score	Airport	Score
Kabul	3.0	Zaranj	2.4
Jalalabad	2.4	Farah	2.0
Khost/Salerno	2.4	Herat	1.4
Ghazni	2.3	Qala-e-Naw	1.2
Uruzgan	2.4	Mazar-e-Sharif	1.2
Kandahar	3.2	Kunduz	1.3
Lashkar Gah	3.3	Bamyan	1.1

Source: Exclusive Analysis

Risks to helicopters are greatest in the east, along the Afghanistan-Pakistan border and in the south; militants are likely to acquire only limited guided surface-to-air missile capabilities.

Risks of militant attacks on military and contractor helicopters over the next year will be greatest in the east in provinces around Kabul (especially Wardak and Logar), along the border with Pakistan and in the south. There have been sporadic militant RPG attacks on coalition helicopters and small arms and RPG attacks on helicopters are likely to increase in the coming year. On 14 July 2009, heavy-calibre machine-gun fire caused a helicopter to crash in

Sangin, Helmand. On 19 August 2009, a UK Chinook helicopter was attacked and made an emergency landing after an engine caught fire. We expect militants in Pakistan's tribal areas to try to acquire surface-to-air missiles (SAM) in order to target the greater number of US helicopters that will be in operation, raising risks to aircraft flying below 10,000 feet along the Pakistan-Afghanistan border. If militants were to acquire heat-seeking SAMs, helicopter shoot down risks would substantially increase. However, militants are likely to require state backing to acquire the number of SAMs, training and logistic support needed to cause critical damage to coalition operations, which neither Pakistan, Iran nor India (the three best-placed potential suppliers) are likely to provide. This means that militants are likely to acquire at most a very limited number of SAMs, given the cost of third-generation SAMs and the training needed to use them effectively.

Oil and gas fields located in Jawzjan and Sari Pul provinces where the Taliban are weak face limited risks of attack, although insurgents' efforts to target energy assets are likely to increase over the coming three years as exploration gets under way.

Afghanistan has four proven natural gas fields in Jawzjan province and three proven oilfields in Sari Pul, including the Angoat oilfield, the only field that has had sustained production. In September 2009, Afghanistan ended its first bidding round for exploration and production sharing contracts in three oil and gas blocks. Northern Afghanistan will most probably be the least violent region in the country in 2010. This is primarily because powerful local warlords and the non-Pashtun population have been largely able to repel Taliban attempts to re-establish control. Attacks on government and coalition assets are likely to rise in Faryab province, but will have limited impact on neighbouring Sari Pul and Jawzjan provinces. Oil and gas projects are likely to be well-secured, but insurgent efforts to target these projects will most probably increase over the next three years, as exploration expands. Such attacks are most likely to take the form of perimeter bombings or kidnap or killing of personnel.

Aid workers face increasing risks of attack and kidnapping for ransom, especially in Kabul; risks of attacks along roads are likely to increase in the south and the east.

While the majority of militant attacks will be directed against coalition and Afghan security forces, aid workers face increasing risks of attack and kidnapping for ransom, particularly in and around Kabul. In October 2008, a Dutch and a Canadian journalist were kidnapped near Kabul and a female aid worker at Serving Emergency Relief and Vocational Enterprise (SERVE) was killed. In November 2008, also in Kabul, a French aid worker was kidnapped. Foreign NGO staff are most likely to be targeted while travelling by road to their offices and at unsecured residences, located mostly in Shar-e-Now, Wazir Akbar Khan and Sher Pur districts. Our sources report that Taliban and criminal groups have made the distinction between black UN lettering on vehicles (indicating political operations) and the blue UN lettering (indicating humanitarian operations), to focus kidnapping for ransom attacks on humanitarian workers. Aid workers are also vulnerable to attack at hotels and restaurants catering to foreigners in the Wazir Akbar Khan district. Sporadic bomb attacks and opportunistic kidnappings targeting aid workers are likely to continue in the west. Kidnapping for ransom by criminal groups is likely to increase in the north and central regions where coalition forces have a weaker presence. Attacks on NGOs still operating in the south and the east are likely to rise along with increasing attacks targeting US troop deployments, especially along roads.

2. The Politics of Investment Reform in India

The Congress Party's success in the May 2009 elections ended its dependence on the Left political parties that resisted liberalisation and privatisation policies during the previous term. The Congress-led United Progressive Alliance (UPA) government now has both the parliamentary seats, and electoral mandate, to implement its reform plans for tax policy and investment regulations governing the infrastructure, insurance, banking, retail and energy sectors. This article forecasts which reforms are likely to pass in 2010, where political and popular opposition will probably derail proposals, and what the implications are for foreign investors.

The two main opposition groups, the Bharatiya Janata Party (BJP) and the Left parties, are unlikely to pose any significant threat to the stability of the Congress-led UPA coalition.

The BJP is currently experiencing a crisis of senior leadership. Several leaders such as Jaswant Singh, Yashwant Sinha and Arun Shourie, have been criticising party policies that they claim were responsible for the 2009 defeat. The BJP's leader and former prime ministerial candidate, Lal Krishna Advani, is likely to step down from his role as opposition leader in Parliament. Party President Rajnath Singh is also expected to resign in 2010, with more moderate leaders like Sushma Swaraj and Arun Jaitley taking over. The BJP will however challenge government reforms in the retail and banking sectors in 2010. Furthermore, the BJP's ability to oppose reform, particularly in energy policy, is likely to increase in 2011-14, as controversial leaders step down and the party recovers some of its voting base.

The Left parties, most significantly the Communist Party of India (Marxist), lost over two-thirds of their seats in the Lower House of Parliament. The Left parties support the rural poor, in particular land rights, and small local businesses. They are also vocal on banking reform. They are most likely to exert influence only at state level, particularly in West Bengal and Kerala. These states have shown increasing interest in attracting greater foreign investment in manufacturing, infrastructure and services, but are unwilling to offer special incentives to foreign investors.

The UPA coalition will be led initially by 77-year old Prime Minister Manmohan Singh.

However, Rahul Gandhi, the son of Congress President Sonia Gandhi, will probably play an increasingly active role in formulating policy in the UPA government, in preparation to succeed Singh in 2013-14. Other key architects of the reform programme are Finance Minister Pranab Mukherjee and the deputy commissioner of the Planning Commission Montek Singh Ahluwalia.

The government is likely to have a fair degree of success in reforming policies related to infrastructure spending, tax and the insurance sector.

Infrastructure

Dispute resolution mechanisms and bidding procedures are likely to be improved incrementally, but project risks will not decrease significantly in the next three years.

Infrastructure constraints, particularly in roads and telecommunications, are a significant impediment to growth in India and thus a key focus of the Singh government. The government aims to increase investment in infrastructure from the current 4.6% to 8% of GDP by 2012, primarily through public-private partnerships. The new Road Transport Minister Kamal Nath has pledged to construct 7,000km of highways in 2010, for which significant foreign investment is being sought, in addition to a $3 billion World Bank loan.

A key proposed reform is to streamline the bidding process to three stages and cut approval and contract agreement times to 18 months. The only opposition to increasing private participation in infrastructure comes from the Left parties which are unlikely to influence infrastructure reforms significantly.

Contract frustration and project delay risks are significant, however. Once projects begin, operators and banks technically have access to international arbitration mechanisms, but infrastructure contracts have been terminated with little notice in the past. A new Dispute Resolution Board, which would be set up under the authority of the National Highways Authority of India, will have the mandate to streamline dispute mechanism cases. This would then be taken to district-level courts to be adjudicated if necessary.

Tax Code

Certain proposals for tax reform threaten the existing tax assumptions for foreign investors.

The most radical proposed change is the redefinition of an 'Indian resident company' from the existing nomenclature of the 1961 Income Tax Act, to one where any company whose management is 'partially located' in India at any time of the year would be treated as an Indian firm (and thus required to pay taxes accordingly).

In this case, the company would be taxed on income that is derived outside India for the sale of assets or services that may be rendered outside India.

This provision has already elicited significant opposition from Indian corporate bodies such as the Confederation of Indian Industry, and we expect greater clarity over its provisions during the course of the debate over the tax code in Parliament.

The new tax code will supersede existing double taxation avoidance treaties with countries such as Mauritius and Switzerland, through which several foreign companies route their investments to claim tax benefits. This is likely to impact on investors in the power, infrastructure, mining and energy sectors who often take this route to invest in India.

The direct tax code, however, does contain positive indicators to incentivise investment in specific sectors. It would replace profit-linked incentives with a provision to allow any capital expenditure as deductible expenditure. Losses will also be allowed to be 'carried forward' for taxation purposes until they are completely absorbed. These incentives are specifically targeted at businesses in the infrastructure, power, mining and energy sectors.

Insurance

Insurance sector reform permitting greater foreign direct investment (FDI) is likely in 2010.

Insurance in India is still dominated by the state-owned Life Insurance Corporation of India, which has a 62% market share. The other state-owned insurers are New India Assurance, Oriental Insurance, National Insurance and United India Insurance companies. There are currently 36 private insurance companies with operations in India, with foreign representation from AIG, New York Life and Allianz who operate in partnerships with Indian companies.

We expect the Insurance Laws Amendment Bill to be presented in the Lower House of Parliament for approval in 2010. This bill proposes an increase in the ceiling on FDI in insurance from the current 26% to 49%. It would also allow foreign re-insurers to establish operations in India. Currently, only the state-run Government Insurance Corporation is allowed to do so. Reforms to permit FDI in insurance are expected to attract $2 billion annually.

The BJP supports the insurance bill. Potential opposition from state-owned insurers will be mitigated by the fact that they will still be exempted from the 10.3% service tax for health insurance provision in the rural areas (giving them an advantage over private companies). The Left parties oppose the bill, preferring to restrict insurance provision by non-government players. However, given how much the Left parties have been weakened, we do not expect delays to the passage of this bill.

We also anticipate that the government will sell minority stakes in state-run insurance companies, such as New India Assurance, to domestic investors. We expect domestic private companies to be favoured to purchase these stakes, given that these companies are considered key national brands.

While the government is discussing reforms in the banking, retail and energy sectors, most are unlikely to pass in 2010 given significant opposition. Moves to permit greater foreign investment in these sectors are likely to be slow beyond 2010.

Banking

The government is trying to merge some state-run banks and raise foreign ownership thresholds in private banks; progress is likely to be slow.

The reform agenda of the Indian government

Sector	Reform	Likelihood of Implementation
Infrastructure	Streamline bidding process to 3 sages and cut approval time to 18 months	Likely in 2010
	Faster Dispute Resolution Mechanisms	Likely in 2010
Taxation	Redefine an "Indian resident company" so more firms can pay tax on foreign-earned income	Modifications and comes in April 2011
	Better investment incentives re: treatment of capital expenditure and carrying losses forward	Comes in April 2011
Insurance	Raising the limit on FDI from 26% to 49%	Likely in 2010
	Allow foreign reinsurers to establish operations	Likely in 2010
	Government to sell its minority interests	Likely in 2010
Banking	Raise the current 74% FDI limit	Likely in this Parliament
	Merge small public banks but keep majority government ownership	Likely in 2010
	New barriers to foreign banks opening branches	Probably resolved in 2010
Retail	Increase 51% FDI limit for single brand retailers	Likely beyond 2011
	More foreign-local partnerships for logistical and wholesale operations	Likely by mid-2010
	Unrestricted multi-brand retail operations	Likely after 2011
Energy	Auction of up to 70 oil and gas blocks	Happens in 2010
	Partial privatisation of Coal Authority of India	Happens in 2010
	Some upward revision of gas prices to attract E&P	Likely in 2010
	Retail oil price de-regulation	Restricted implementation likely after 2010
	Allow 49% FDI in nuclear power	Restricted foreign participation likely instead

Source: Exclusive Analysis

State-run banks dominate in India and they can expect government backing if they face any strains on their capital adequacy ratios. In September 2009, the government obtained a $2 billion loan from the World Bank to recapitalise government-run banks. This disbursal was made as a Development Policy Loan, reducing the conditionalities otherwise associated with such a loan.

The government wants to merge public banks since the smaller ones are under-capitalised and unable to provide meaningful amounts of credit to large corporations. An important element of proposed banking sector reform is therefore the merger of several state-run banks, particularly affiliates of the State Bank of India (SBI); the State Bank of Indore will probably be the first to be merged with the SBI. This initiative does not suggest that the government will reduce its stake below 51% in public banks however.

There is considerable opposition to increasing the 74% FDI threshold in private banks. This opposition spreads across the Left, elements within the Congress Party and the employees of public banks. Indeed, employees of public banks are strongly unionised and very likely to resort to coordinated national-level strikes if greater FDI is permitted in banking. This opposition is only expected to slow down the implementation of reform, not block it. So while we do not expect an increase in the 74% ceiling in 2010, it is likely to happen at some point later in the UPA's term.

The Indian government is also likely to impose some restrictions on foreign banks opening new branches in India in 2010, as it claims that Indian banks are discriminated against abroad. We expect this to be resolved in the one-year outlook though, reducing the risks of a systemic blocking of foreign banks' operations in India.

Retail

The UPA government is unlikely to permit FDI in direct retail operations in 2010.

Small cash-and-carry shops control over 95% of India's $350 billion retail industry and firmly oppose the presence of foreign players. The UPA government, in its first term, indicated that it would permit FDI in this sector, with some constraints. These included a ban on foreign retailers opening shops selling brands from a range of manufacturers. While the exit of the Left from power has largely removed parliamentary opposition to FDI in retail, we still do not expect a significant opening up of the sector in 2010.

Currently, 51% FDI is permitted in single-brand retail in India, permitting foreign retailers to set up shops in India through local franchises. We expect greater FDI to be permitted in single-brand retail, though this would likely be conditional upon these retailers sourcing a proportion of their goods from Indian vendors.

We do though expect foreign retailers to be increasingly allowed to form partnerships with local firms for logistical and wholesale operations. Indeed, Wal-Mart has already been allowed to enter into an operational alliance with Indian Bharti Enterprises for retail operations. Prominent multinational retailers such as France's Carrefour and the UK's Tesco have also expressed an interest in retailing operations in India, and they are likely to begin wholesale and logistical operations in 2010. Tesco, which has partnered with India's Tata Group, and Carrefour, which is in talks with Pantaloon, are likely to begin wholesale operations in India by mid 2010.

We point out that they would still be unable to operate as direct retailers (i.e. set up shops catering directly to retail customers). The Parliamentary Standing

Committee on Commerce has also recommended a National Shopping Mall Regulation Act that would restrict the ability of foreign companies to establish shopping malls, though this is not likely to be passed in 2010 due to opposition to the measure within Congress.

Energy

The government is likely to delay divesting its stakes in energy companies.

The Congress government is keen to attract foreign participation in domestic oil and gas exploration as it seeks to cut the dependence on imports, which currently amount to 65% of oil supply. Its auction of up to 70 oil and gas blocks for exploration is expected to attract over $5 billion of investment. Cairn Energy (UK), Gazprom (Russia), Mosbacher Energy (US) and Total (France) are some of the multinational energy companies with a presence in India. While the government is actively soliciting foreign investment in oil and gas exploration, it is still unlikely to dilute its stakes in key oil and gas exploration companies significantly given the sector's strategic importance. In 2010, we do though expect to see a partial sale in the Coal Authority of India.

Gas prices were last revised in 2005 and will probably be revised again in 2010.

The government wants to attract greater investment in gas exploration to supply the fertiliser and power industries. Given this, we expect companies to be allowed some freedom to sell gas at prices slightly above current prices. They will not be free though to sell gas wholly at market rates, despite the allowance of 100% FDI in the sector. Since the fertiliser and power provision industries depend heavily on natural gas, we expect the government to subsidise prices for extraction by state-run companies.

Meaningful cuts to retail energy subsidies are unlikely in 2010.

The BJP and Congress are inclined to support energy sector reform. Indeed, the BJP had created the Department of Disinvestment when it was in power, to speed up reforms and remove government control from loss-making state-run companies. However, the fuel prices that the public pay are heavily subsidised in India. Even small price increases of retail fuel typically result in national protests and are often raised as campaign issues in state elections. The BJP has consistently opposed every price increase in retail prices the Congress government has made. Petroleum Minister Murli Deora announced the establishment of a government committee to study the scope of aligning domestic oil prices with global crude prices in the 2009 budget, but such a change would be unlikely in 2010 given the probable negative public reaction that would ensue over the prices of essential commodities.

We expect to see continued resistance to permitting foreign investment in nuclear power.

Apart from petroleum, Prime Minister Singh has identified nuclear energy as a key component of India's energy policy, and wants to increase production by 2020. While the signing of nuclear energy agreements with the US, Russia and France has opened up opportunities for foreign investors, we do not expect the proposed amendment to the Atomic Energy Act permitting 49% FDI in the sector to come into force in 2010. The primary deterrent for greater foreign investment is the government's insistence that any foreign operator must agree to assume liability for an accident at a nuclear power station for which it supplied equipment, or for one with which it has a maintenance agreement. Also, the government has shown indications that it favours enhancing domestic investment in the sector, with L&T and Tata Power already having expressed interest in investing in nuclear power plants. We do though expect continued participation by nuclear power companies from Canada, the US (including Westinghouse) and France (Areva) in India, as the government dismantles the monopoly of the state-run Nuclear Power Corporation of India (NPCIL). This policy is designed to obtain much-needed foreign nuclear technology and overcome supply constraints on domestic producers.

3. Pakistan in 2010: New Alliances, New Risks?

Understanding the risks to assets and individuals in Pakistan requires a detailed analysis of the significance of certain groups and political actors, and the direct and indirect implications of their activities. In this article we consider the capability and motivation of the Pakistan-Taliban to launch attacks against different target sets within Pakistan; the coordination between FATA-, Kashmir- and Punjab-based militant groups and how this is leading to increased risks; the ISI's declining ability to influence militant groups; anti-Pashtun unrest in urban areas and the possibility of attacks in India by Pakistan-based militants leading to renewed military confrontation between the two countries.

The Pakistan-Taliban are likely to expand in strength and reach in 2010, but internal divisions and their greater focus on extending influence in the tribal areas mean that they are unlikely to pose a viable challenge to the integrity of the Pakistani state.

The Pakistan-Taliban operate separately from the Afghan-Taliban, although they share some aims, notably the removal of Western military forces from Afghanistan and the wish to secure their own areas of territorial control against interference from Pakistan's central government or US drone strikes. They are made up of several units and their operations expand across Pakistan's Federally Administered Tribal Areas (FATA) and North West Frontier Province (NWFP). However, the Pakistan-Taliban lack a cohesive internal agenda beyond these broad goals.

The nominal head of the Afghan-Taliban, Mullah Omar, is thought to be in hiding in Quetta, Baluchistan, very likely with the knowledge of Pakistan's Inter-Services Intelligence (ISI), which is the main intelligence agency in

143

Pakistan. The ISI's policy-planning assumption is that NATO will leave Afghanistan in three to five years and that Northern Alliance Tajiks, under the influence of India, will hold sway in Kabul. The ISI therefore seeks to preserve some influence among the Afghan-Taliban in order to maintain a pro-Pakistan government in Afghanistan.

Mullah Omar opposes terrorist operations within Pakistan, since to do otherwise would threaten his own position. This line is also taken by those Pakistan-Taliban factions that have a history of cooperation with the Pakistani state, such as the Haqqani network based near Miramshah and the Maulvi Nazir-Hafiz Gul Bahadur alliance in North Waziristan. These factions focus almost exclusively on operations within Afghanistan and on the defence of their own territory.

However, Pakistan-Taliban factions such as the Tehreek-e-Taliban Pakistan (TTP) are more likely to consider terrorist attacks in Pakistan in order to force a change in state policy. For all factions, the desire to protect territory and consolidate power in the tribal areas is paramount. It is unlikely at present that any have serious aspirations to take over the Pakistani state, which they would in any case find nearly impossible not only because they are largely Pashtuns and the Pakistani state is dominated by Punjabis but also because of their strict application of sharia law, for which there is not widespread support.

US airstrikes in Pakistan's tribal areas (frequency per month)

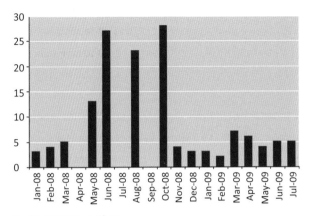

Source: Exclusive Analysis

Over the course of 2010, the pressure brought on by Army operations in FATA is likely to lead to FATA-based militant groups improving their coordination with each other and with Kashmir-based militant groups in order to carry out terrorist attacks on Pakistani cities.

The Army's operations in FATA that began in June 2009 have the limited military objective of neutralising the threat from the TTP and other groups who stage attacks on the state; and the political objective of convincing Western governments, especially the US, that the Pakistani government is serious about acting against Islamist terrorism. However, while the Army is likely to seek to negotiate local peace agreements with individual Pakistan-Taliban leaders (as it has repeatedly done since 2004), its perceived complicity with US drone attacks in FATA and continuing limited offensive operations in selected areas like South Waziristan, are increasingly likely to lead to operational alliances between militants.

While such alliances between militant groups are usually unsustainable beyond a limited timeframe (as illustrated by the breakdown of the three-month-old alliance between the TTP and militant commanders Hafiz Gul Bahadur in North Waziristan and Maulvi Nazir in South Waziristan in the spring of 2009), they are likely to offer significant resistance to the Army. As all militant groups resent the Army's presence in Waziristan, a military effort to form an anti-TTP alliance is likely to meet with only limited success.

The Army's initiation of limited ground operations with renewed air strikes in Waziristan is unlikely to significantly erode militant capability; the operations would at best succeed in clearing key transit routes for militants in FATA.

TTP leader Hakimullah Mehsud has organised an intensification of militant attacks within Pakistan in order to dissuade the Army from launching ground operations in Waziristan. The Army was, however, constrained in expediting its ground offensive in Waziristan following the attack on its General Headquarters in Rawalpindi in October 2009. We do not expect the limited ground operations to significantly erode the ability of TTP fighters to infiltrate Punjab and Sindh. However, some disruption to fighter movement and supplies for the TTP is likely as the Army would be able to capture some transit routes in South Waziristan.

Exclusive Analysis' assessment of released intelligence from militant arrests also indicates an increasing degree of cooperation between the Pakistan-Taliban and Kashmir-based groups such as Lashkar-e-Toiba (LeT) and organisations with mainly ethnic Punjabi fighters such as Lashkar-e-Jhangvi (LeJ). An LeJ militant arrested in connection with the terrorist attack on the Sri Lankan cricket team in Lahore in March 2009 said that he had received operational training and instructions in North Waziristan, where Pakistan-Taliban militants have a significant presence. The suicide car-bombing attack on a market in Kohat, NWFP, in September 2009, was likely to have been carried out by a faction of the Lashkar-e-Jhangvi, whose targets have previously been largely limited to Punjab and Sindh. Such cooperation is likely to increase the reach and scope of terrorist attacks within Pakistan in the coming year.

'Crescent of Influence' - Convergence of Pakistani Militant Groups

Source: Exclusive Analysis

Pakistan-Taliban militants, particularly the TTP network, are increasingly likely to cooperate with other militant groups in FATA to stage attacks in Pakistani cities. The killing of TTP leader Baitullah Mehsud has fragmented the command structure but it is unlikely to reduce their capability to stage attacks outside FATA.

The TTP's primary aim is to end the Pakistani government's support for NATO operations in Afghanistan and seek an end to continuing US drone attacks in FATA that target its leadership, and it is likely to keep up its strategy of mounting terrorist attacks within Pakistan to achieve this objective. TTP fighters (estimated at up to 10,000) have relatively little difficulty moving into Pakistani cities. The bomb attack on the Pearl Continental Hotel on 9 June 2009 was most likely facilitated by the TTP.

While the killing of Baitullah Mehsud in a drone strike in August 2009 has already led to some fragmentation of command, funding and loss of capability within the TTP, it is highly likely that the network will remain operative and will engage in revenge attacks. While Mehsud's death was followed by infighting for succession, this was motivated not by a difference over objectives but the fact that leadership of the TTP would bring with it attractive negotiating leverage with Pakistan's Army and government. Indeed, the attack on a crowded market in Kohat, NWFP, in September 2009 was likely facilitated by the TTP. While risks are particularly significant in Peshawar, the influx of Pashtun fighters from FATA also raises risks in Karachi and other major cities such as Islamabad and Lahore. Government, defence and police buildings will be the primary targets, and attacks on aid agencies (as illustrated by the suicide bombing in the UN office in Islamabad in October 2009) and public transport will also likely increase.

The ISI's influence over militant groups active in Pakistan is probably being eroded, which will limit its ability to inform counterterrorist activity in Pakistani cities.

The ability of the ISI to monitor and control terrorist networks within Pakistan is probably being eroded, especially in the NWFP and tribal areas. The ISI disagreed with Military Intelligence over the extent of military operations in

Swat. The ISI has an interest to ensure that some militant capability remains so that it could be directed towards India in case of renewed conflict; this interest would be at odds with a complete eradication of militant groups such as Lashkar-e-Toiba (LeT) and Jaish-e-Mohammed (JeM) who are also probably coming under increasing influence from the Pakistan-Taliban. Following the 2008 Mumbai terrorist attacks, JeM leader Masood Azhar relocated to Waziristan where he is almost certainly being sheltered by the TTP to avoid arrest by Pakistani security forces. The ISI's understanding of the complex and multi-layered relationships between militant groups and individuals in the tribal areas is only partial, undermining its ability to direct and curtail groups' activities. This is also likely to impact negatively on the ISI's ability to inform effective counterterrorism operations in Pakistan and disrupt attack plots before they reach execution.

Attacks by Pakistan-Taliban and al-Qaeda militants on government and civilian targets in major Pakistani cities, alongside frustration over poor state service provision, leads to a risk of anti-Pashtun unrest across Pakistan, particularly in Karachi.

While there is broad sympathy across Pakistan for the plight of displaced civilians from Swat, in Sindh, nationalist parties such as Jeay Sindh Qaumi Mahaz (JSQM) and the Muttahida Qaumi Movement (MQM), which represents Mohajir in Sindh, are likely to fuel anti-Pashtun sentiments. Indeed in Karachi, in particular, there is an increasing suspicion of Pashtuns, who as an ethnic community, are being viewed as responsible for carrying out most terrorist attacks in Pakistan. This will increase the likelihood of smaller incidents triggering large-scale unrest. This is particularly true in places where there are existing ethnic fault-lines that have also become attached to political affiliation, such as Karachi where the Pashtun and majority Mohajir and Sindhi populations regularly confront each other in response to local or national incidents. In April 2009, fighting between activists of the MQM and Pashtuns lasted over three days, leaving over 29 local residents dead, including MQM activists and Pashtun civilians. The paramilitary Sindh Rangers were deployed on the streets of Karachi to disperse the protesters. Protests in Karachi can turn violent with little notice, and are likely to result in property damage to commercial establishments and vehicles. Risks of violence in Pashtun-dominated areas of Karachi such as Sher-e-Faisal and Gulshan-e-Hadeed are particularly noteworthy.

Risk-Rated Map of Pakistan from Country Risk Evaluation and Assessment Model (6 October 2009)

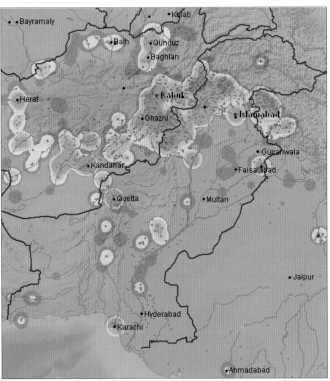

Source: Exclusive Analysis

Some Pakistan-based militants will almost certainly be planning major terrorist attacks on India, hoping to cause the Pakistan Army to redeploy troops away from FATA to the border or to prompt India to respond militarily.

As Pakistan-Taliban militants come under pressure from Army operations in FATA, they have an increasing interest in sponsoring an attack on India to escalate war risks, which would probably lead to a halt in military operations in Waziristan. While the Pakistan-Taliban have no demonstrated infrastructure or local cells in India, they have probably increased their influence among Kashmir-focused groups such as LeT and JeM who have an interest in provoking an Indian reaction. This, coupled with the probable declining influence of the ISI over LeT, increases the risk of a major terrorist attack on an Indian city in 2010.

An Islamist terrorist attack would be likely to lead to only a limited military reprisal by India, who, under US pressure, would likely moderate their response.

Given the increased strength of the Congress Party following the May 2009 elections, Indian Prime Minister Singh will almost certainly resist any political pressure for a full-scale military incursion into Pakistan in the event of a terrorist attack. India's willingness to resume ministerial-level talks with Pakistan and its acceptance of the trial of Mumbai attacks suspects in Pakistani courts have decreased war risks to date. The meeting between Prime Minister Singh and Pakistani President Zardari in June 2009 resulted in a greater bilateral willingness to negotiate over Kashmir and defence-related issues. However, an attack in an Indian city that was planned in Pakistan would test this resolve severely. Unless Pakistan is seen to deliver on at least some of India's key demands (such as the re-arrest of LeT leader Hafeez Mohammed Saeed) it would be very difficult for India not to respond militarily against Pakistan.

The most likely Indian response to a terrorist attack would be limited air, and possibly special forces, strikes on selected militant targets in Pakistan-administered Kashmir. The Indian government almost certainly realises that any large-scale use of force would provoke a similar response, with risks of escalation increasing subsequently. Pakistan is also unlikely to seek an escalation of the conflict outside of Kashmir. The importance of Karachi port for NATO operations in Afghanistan means that the US would be very likely to pressurise India to avoid a blockade of the port. Prime Minister Singh is also unlikely to risk such an escalatory move, and we assess that he will probably be willing to expend political capital to improve relations with Pakistan.

4. Eurasia and Western Europe

1. China's Challenges in Central Asia: Implications for Investors

China faces a diverse risk environment for its investments in natural resources projects in Kazakhstan, Turkmenistan and Uzbekistan, where it is becoming a dominant player. This article looks at the extent of Chinese investment in Central Asian energy development. It highlights how political considerations are likely to impact on China's existing and new projects in the region, and by extension the interests of Western energy majors and Russia.

China's investments in Central Asia have given it access to large new supplies of oil and natural gas in the area. Furthermore, China's investment in transnational pipelines also provides alternative over-ground access to Middle Eastern oil and gas deposits. Its investment supports Central Asian states financially and operationally and it also ties Central Asian hydrocarbon producers to China via long-term contracts.

Kazakhstan

Kazakhstan has welcomed Chinese investment to balance the dominance of Western energy majors and increase its leverage with Russia.

Kazakhstan's major production-sharing agreements (PSAs like Tengiz, Kashagan and Karachaganak) are with Western companies. However, Chinese investors have gradually acquired a growing share of production since first entering Kazakhstan in 1997, when China National Petroleum Corporation (CNPC) purchased Aktobemunaigaz. Other key upstream acquisitions in the past three years have been Petrokazakhstan (2006) and a 49% share in Mangistaumunaigaz (MMG) in August 2009. Overall, Chinese state-owned majors extracted 15 million tons of Kazakh oil in 2008, almost all by CNPC and affiliated entities. China now controls 21% of all oil production in Kazakhstan, compared to 29% controlled by US majors, 9% by Russian state-owned firms, and 31% by state-owned Kazakh entities.

Kazakhstan is also keen to attract financing from Chinese sovereign wealth funds in order to help finance its continuing acquisitions in its own domestic downstream sector. China Investment Corporation's acquisition of 11% of Kazmunaigaz's Global Depository Receipts for $939 million in September 2009 is an example of this.

China's growing presence has strengthened Kazakhstan's negotiating position with Russia, particularly over Kazakh gas exports and joint projects in the downstream sector. Kazakhstan's need for leverage over Russia was a factor in its awarding a stake in MMG to CNPC. This said, Kazakhstan is likely to introduce new tougher labour regulations in its domestic energy industry due to increasing numbers of Chinese migrant workers.

China is unlikely to receive preferential treatment in tenders for Kazakhstan's offshore deposits in the northern part of the Caspian Sea.

Kazakhstan aims to expand its downstream presence in Europe. It will probably therefore trade some of its offshore reserves in exchange for the downstream assets of European partners. This suggests Western majors, rather than Chinese firms, will gain access to offshore deposits in the Caspian Sea. The recent resumption of negotiations with StatoilHydro for the Abai deposit (760 million tons) is consistent with this. Likewise, in October 2009, France's Total and GDF Suez acquired a share in the Khvalynskoe deposit in exchange for guarantees of $1 billion investment into the development of the field.

Separately, CNPC owns 67% of PetroKazakhstan and 49% of MMG. The Kazakh government is increasing its operations in the domestic downstream sector and has put the Shymkent refinery, which is operated by PetroKazakhstan, on the state's strategic investment list. Both companies are likely to be asked to divert increasing volumes of crude production to this refinery. In addition, they are likely to be forced to sell more oil products in the domestic market in order to reduce Kazakhstan's dependence on gasoline, diesel and jet fuel imports from Russia. Such developments are likely to increase contract delivery and cash flow risks associated with PetroKazakhstan and MMG.

Turkmenistan

China is heavily involved in onshore gas development in Turkmenistan.

Turkmenistan has traditionally preferred to grant onshore development contracts to relatively small foreign companies (e.g. Burren Energy, Mitro Oil, Dragon Oil and Buried Hill Energy) rather than big multinationals. However, the Bagtyiarlyk deposits in the southeast are expected to be a major resource base for Turkmen gas exports to China starting in 2010. Given their strategic importance, Turkmenistan therefore signed a PSA with CNPC in July 2007 to develop the deposits. The two sides are projecting an increase in Turkmen supplies to 40 billion cubic metres (bcm) a year by 2015-20 as CNPC has now also pledged a $3 billion investment into Turkmenistan's largest South Yolotan field.

Turkmenistan is likely to grant most new offshore contracts to Western and Russian companies.

Germany's RWE and Russia's Itera have already been granted offshore contracts, and President Berdimukhamedov's recent meetings with US officials indicate that the government would like to see multinational players such as ExxonMobil and Chevron developing these fields. If natural gas discoveries in offshore fields prove sufficient, Turkmenistan has indicated that it would join the EU-lobbied Nabucco pipeline.

The country also intends to increase its oil production significantly once most of the 31 offshore fields start operating. According to Turkmenistan's new hydrocarbon law (2008), the only fixed tax rate will be a 20% profit tax throughout the contract period. Bonuses and royalties will be negotiated on an individual basis. Turkmenistan will not only grant PSAs but will also enter joint ventures with foreign operators, as well as sign concession agreements with an option of 10 years instead of 5 as previously.

Uzbekistan

Uzbekistan's wish to diversify its gas export outlets has increased risks for Russian firms and favoured CNPC.

Major foreign operators in Uzbekistan are Russia's Lukoil and Gazprom, China's CNPC and Malaysia's Petronas. Russian firm Lukoil's contract for its Khauzak PSA stipulated that a foreign investor needs to recoup its costs before sharing revenues with the government. However, Lukoil has been forced to share gas with the Uzbek government from the start of the project, something that Lukoil contests.

In contrast, several new projects involving CNPC face lower contract risks due to Uzbekistan's aim to diversify its export outlets similarly to what Kazakhstan and Turkmenistan have done. CNPC's interests include the following.

• In October 2008, CNPC signed a contract to develop gas at the Mingbulak deposit in Namangan province jointly with Uzbek firms.

• CNPC is a 20% shareholder in Aral project, which a consortium of international investors signed with the Uzbek government in 2006 for 35 years.

• CNPC has signed agreements on geological studies and exploration for Ferghana, Bukhara-Khiva and Ustyurt deposits with national company Uzbekneftegaz.

Amendments to the Uzbek Tax Code significantly decrease tax benefits for foreign operators under PSAs from 2010 onwards.

The government's finances are under considerable pressure and it needs to inject additional capital into the banking system. Therefore, foreign operators will now have to pay profit tax, land tax, tax on water usage and unified social payment at the same rates as domestic companies pay (unless these tax rates are specified in an initial PSA, which is unchangeable). There is a new 25% excise tax for exporters and royalty payments have increased from the previous 4.1% to 30%.

Uzbek authorities aim to increase hydrocarbons production and are dissatisfied about the pace of activities at certain PSA fields such as Mingbulak, Aral and others in Bukhara-Khiva and Ustyurt. CNPC has concentrated its Central Asian investments mainly on developing fields in Kazakhstan and Turkmenistan, rather than Uzbekistan. This raises risks for CNPC in Uzbekistan.

Natural resource deposits in Central Asia

Kazakhstan, Turkmenistan and Uzbekistan have large reserves of hydrocarbons and uranium, and Tajikistan's mountain rivers are yet to be harnessed for electricity generation.

Official statistics indicate that **Kazakhstan**'s proven oil deposits stand at 37 billion barrels and that its gas reserves are 3.3 trillion cubic metres (tcm), but other estimates vary. Recent exploratory work along the Caspian shelf suggests that substantial gas deposits (of 6-8 tcm) are yet to be extracted in the Kazakh sector of the Caspian Sea. Kazakhstan is also home to 18% of global reserves of uranium (approximately 800,000 tonnes), a vital component in the generation of nuclear energy.

According to recent data, **Turkmenistan** sits atop the world's third-largest gas reserves. In October 2008, independent auditors Gaffney, Cline & Associates announced that the Southern Yolotan-Osman gas fields in southeast Turkmenistan (Mary region) contain 6 tcm of proven reserves. BP had previously estimated Turkmenistan's gas reserves at 2.9 tcm and the Turkmen government at 24.6 tcm. Dovletabad (1.3 tcm) and Yashlar (700 bcm) are among other significant gas fields in the country. Like Kazakhstan's offshore oilfields in the Caspian, most of Turkmenistan's gas fields are technically complex. For instance, extraction at the Southern Yolotan gas deposit is complicated by the fact that highly pressurised gas is located deep under the soil and salt deposits.

Uzbekistan is also home to substantial natural gas reserves, estimated at 2 tcm. Until the late 1980s, 10% of all Soviet gas production took place in Uzbekistan. The country's gas deposits are situated in southern, central and western parts of the country, particularly in the Kashkadarya (Shurtanskoe and Urga deposits) and Ustyurt provinces.

Tajikistan is home to 14% of the world's proven uranium reserves and to largely undeveloped potential for hydropower generation. Currently, Tajikistan is using approximately only 5% of its hydropower capacity. The country's total capacity is estimated at 527 billion kWhrs. Of this total, 200 billion kWhrs can be harnessed without causing significant harm to the environment, the country's extensive cotton agriculture and countries located downstream from Taijikistan.

Other Notable Power Projects in Central Asia

Kazakhstan - Kazakhstan's state-owned uranium monopoly, Kazatomprom, signed an agreement with the China Guandong Nuclear Power Corporation in 2007. This was for joint uranium extraction and construction of nuclear reactors. Kazatomprom signed a similar agreement with the China National Nuclear Corporation.

Tajikistan - In 2009, China announced that it will invest $1 billion in developing Tajikistan's energy infrastructure. These funds will mostly be spent on construction of a hydropower plant on the Khingob river, construction of a coal-fired power station in the capital, Dushanbe, and repair of existing energy infrastructure and roads (particularly the Dushanbe-Dangara highway).

Kyrgyzstan - Beijing is committed to constructing a hydropower plant on Sara-Dzhaza in Kyrgyzstan.

Pipelines and Transport Infrastructure in Central Asia

The Turkmenistan-China gas pipeline is almost completed, providing an annual capacity of 40 bcm/annum at an estimated construction cost of $7.3 billion. Work is under way on the Kazakh section of a gas pipeline designed to connect to the Turkmenistan-China pipeline with a total capacity of 10 bcm/annum.

Parallel to an ambitious programme of pipeline construction in Central Asia, China also plans to build extensive railway and road communications in the region. The aim is to connect China's rapidly developing ports along the Pacific coast (Lianyungang, Tianjin and Qingdao) to Turkey and Iran. Construction of a continuous railway line linking the Chinese Pacific coast to Turkey would allow China to transport its exports more easily and in larger quantities to Western consumers. It would also reduce China's dependence on the Russian-operated Trans-Siberian railway line.

Central Asia-China pipelines

Source: Exclusive Analysis

Regional Security

From a domestic security perspective, China's investments give it an important degree of influence over Central Asian republics.

Alongside Russia, China dominates the agenda of the key regional security institution, the Shanghai Cooperation Organisation. This was set up in 2001 as a counterbalance to Western influence after the collapse of the Soviet Union, with Kazakhstan, Kyrgyzstan, Uzbekistan and Tajikistan as members. The Xinjiang Autonomous Region in northwestern China is currently one of Beijing's biggest security problems because of an active Uyghur separatist movement. Xinjiang shares a common border with Kazakhstan, Kyrgyzstan and Tajikistan, and almost half-a-million Uyghurs reside in these Central Asian republics. China's government is worried that Uyghurs might use the Ferghana Valley in Central Asia as a training area. There are unconfirmed reports of Uyghur presence in radical organisations, such as the Islamic Jihad Union, which use Pakistan's tribal areas as their base. Beijing views economic relations as a way of advancing security objectives. Notably, Central Asian governments did not officially condemn China's forceful response to Uyghur protests in Urumqi in July 2009. Kyrgyzstan went as far as to ban all protests by over 50,000 Uyghurs residing in the republic.

Russia's Backyard?

Russia will reluctantly tolerate Chinese economic expansion into Central Asia.

Chinese expansion in Central Asia is a major concern for Moscow, which since the early 19th century has considered Central Asia to be within its sphere of influence. The Kazakhstan-China oil pipeline only went ahead after Russia's Gazprom refused to commit funds to the originally planned alternative.

Similarly, Tajikistan and Uzbekistan welcomed Chinese investments after Moscow made it clear that it was either uninterested or unable to commit substantial financial resources to developing energy and road infrastructure in these states.

However, we assess that due to commercial imperatives and its objective of energy security, Moscow will tolerate China's expansion in Central Asia. Russia wants to lock European energy firms into long-term contracts. To increase its leverage, Russia's government goes to great lengths to demonstrate that Russian oil and gas can easily end up in Chinese hands. Ongoing construction of the Eastern Siberia-Pacific Ocean oil pipeline (with an annual projected capacity of 80 million tons/annum), with an extension into China, is part of this effort. Similarly, the April 2009 Sino-Russian agreement commits Rosneft and Transneft to supply 15 million tons of oil to China annually over 20 years in exchange for a $25 billion loan.

In 2008, China became Russia's most important trade partner for the first time when bilateral trade volumes reached $57 billion. Despite Russia's complicated investment environment, Chinese businesses have been spending actively in Siberia and in Russia's major cities over the last three years. Between January and September 2009 alone, Chinese investors committed $17 billion to projects in Russia. Much of this money was spent on logging, mineral extraction, infrastructure development and construction. Russia can therefore ill afford a worsening of relations with China.

2. Back with a Bang? Right-Wing Extremism in the US and Western Europe

Right-wing extremism (any combination of extreme nationalism, isolationism, racism, white supremacism, anti-Semitism, and hostility to Islam) has gained traction in Western Europe and the US, in part due to rising unemployment, disaffection with established political parties and perceived favouritism to immigrants and other minority groups. While many people with variations on these views operate within the political process, others undertake violent protests and terrorist or criminal attacks, with a recent phenomenon of left-wing counter-demonstrations and rioting. In this piece we consider the historical trends and the implications for the type, severity and frequency of violence in the US and Western Europe.

Right-wing Extremism in Western Europe

Several far-right political parties in Western Europe achieved notable electoral success in 2009 due in part to economic dissatisfaction and debates on policies on minorities and immigration.

In Western Europe, far-right political parties have sought to capitalise on voter disaffection with established political parties, the handling of the economic crisis, rising unemployment and hostility to immigrants (in many cases Muslim immigrants in particular) to increase their popular support. They achieved success in the UK, Netherlands and Austria in the June 2009 European Parliament elections. Specifically, the Party for Freedom (PVV) won 16.9% of the vote (the second highest share of the vote among Dutch parties), and the Freedom Party for Austria (FPO) won 12.7% (the fourth highest share of the vote among Austrian parties). The British National Party (BNP) won 8.3% of the vote (the fifth highest share of the vote among UK parties). In addition to these parties, there are many other far-right political parties in Western Europe that have received less electoral support than the PVV, FPO and BNP. These include the National Democratic Party (NPD) in Germany (who won 4.3% of the vote in national elections), Forza Nuova in Italy (who won 2%), and the People's Front in Sweden (which came into existence in November 2008 as the successor organisation for the National Socialist Front, whose best result was less than 0.1% in national elections in 2006). In addition to these political parties, there are also formal protest groups, such as the English Defence League in the UK.

Far-right protest groups have recently tended to demonstrate against Islam and against left-wing rallies and events. In the UK and Germany in particular, some of the protests have prompted counter-demonstrations, triggering communal violence, rioting and property damage.

Although many far-right political parties have policy positions on EU membership, tax and social services and other economic issues, it is noteworthy that most of the violent protests by and against far-right parties have tended to be around Islam or minority groups, rather than economic issues. In the UK, right-wing groups have begun a campaign against what they term 'Muslim extremism' after a protest by followers of former al-Muhajiroun leader Omar Bakri Mohammed during a welcome-home parade for British soldiers in Luton in March 2009. Playing on fears of Islam in the UK, groups like the English Defence League have staged protests in an attempt to mobilise larger numbers of people. In September 2009, fighting between riot police and around 100 right-wing protesters broke out in Birmingham during a rally organised by the English Defence League, and there has been rioting and property damage, including an arson attack on an Islamic centre in Luton in May 2009. In turn, these right-wing rallies have provoked counter-demonstrations by left-wing activists (such as Unite Against Fascism) and Muslim youths. Similarly, in Germany, right-wing groups, such as the NPD, have organised numerous demonstrations in 2009. In September 2009, 90 NPD activists protested in Hamburg against a left-wing street festival that was to be held there the following day. The rally was disrupted by approximately 2,700 anti-fascist protesters, prompting fighting between rival demonstrators and with riot police, with some minor damage to nearby vehicles. There have been several other protests against far-right parties in Germany, including against an NPD conference in Berlin in April 2009 and against an anti-Islam conference organised by several European far-right parties in September 2008 in Cologne. Similarly in Venlo, Netherlands, some 60 people were detained during a rally of the rightist Dutch People's Union; some 100 people held a counter-rally and scuffled with the police.

Over the past decade, the trend towards racially and religiously motivated violence has increased across most of Western Europe.

Beyond the political process and public protests, there is also evidence of an increase in right-wing attacks, for example hate crimes and terror plots. It may be that the electoral gains of right-wing parties have emboldened some of their supporters to undertake acts of violence; alternatively, it may be that the same underlying conditions that delivered electoral success to parties has triggered a separate set of individuals to shun the political process and undertake violence instead. Most Western European countries do not keep sufficient data to compare trends in right-wing violence, but of those that do (Austria, Germany, France and Sweden), Germany has both the highest absolute number of incidents (17,176 in 2007) and the highest rate of increase from 2001-07 (71%). The German Interior Ministry reported in April 2009 that overall politically motivated offences in Germany rose 11.4% from 2001-08 to 31,801, and right-wing extremist attacks increased 19% beyond the 2007 figures to 20,422.

According to the 2009 Annual Report of the European Union Agency for Fundamental Rights, the overall number of recorded racially motivated incidents is much higher in England & Wales than in any other European country, with over 61,000 recorded incidents in 2007 alone, and Germany was second highest, having recorded nearly 18,000 racially motivated crimes in 2007. Scotland reported 4,474 offences in 2007, Sweden reported 2,813 crimes, Belgium reported 1,289 and France reported 707. Among Western European countries for which data was available, the rates of increase have been highest in Belgium (70% 2000-07 year on year), Austria (67%), Finland (41%), England & Wales (29%) and Germany (20% from 2001-07). Anti-Semitic crime has increased most notably in the UK and Austria, with the absolute number of incidents highest in Germany, the UK and France among those Western European countries for which data is available.

In the UK and Germany, right-wing extremists are specifically targeting Muslims and symbols of Islam, among other minority groups.

There have been a number of intercepted plots that sought to target Muslims, some of which had proceeded to acquisition of materials and construction of explosive devices. For instance, in June 2009, a man and his son suspected of being white supremacists, were arrested in County Durham for possessing ricin and were charged with encouraging others to commit attacks. Likewise, in July 2009, a neo-Nazi was convicted of explosives-related offences as part of a plot to attack 'non-British' targets. In the October 2007 arrest of an extremist from East Yorkshire (for having constructed four nail bombs) there was no mention of specific targets, but he had written about starting a racist war in which Muslims and left-wing activists should be attacked and killed. In Germany, there has been a sustained high level of racially motivated arson attacks in the east of the country in particular, mainly committed by members of far-right groups in Saxony-Anhalt and Brandenburg and, to a lesser extent, in Thuringia and Saxony. In March 2007, a mosque under construction in

Berlin-Heinersdorf was set alight by arsonists and a month earlier, a Jewish nursery, also in Berlin, was targeted in a similar attack, most likely by right-wing activists. In 2008, unidentified arsonists set fire to an Islamic prayer room in Aalen, Baden-Württemberg, and in 2009 at least three such attacks had taken place up to October. Many of these incidents appear not to be premeditated. For instance, two football fans confessed to having been intoxicated and trying to set light to a mosque in Stadtallendorf, Hesse, in March 2009. They fired shots at windows after their club, Schalke 04, had lost a football match. The construction of controversial mosques, most notably in Berlin and Cologne, are likely to prompt further attacks on these and similar targets by neo-Nazis, with Molotov cocktails and arson the most likely attack modes.

In the UK and Belgium there has been a greater demonstrated capability, with explosives and weapons seizures as well as efforts to recruit, sometimes successfully, from the armed forces.

In Germany, the majority of attacks have been arson and assault, though in January 2009, the police in the state of Lower Saxony seized some 12 rifles, guns and munitions from far-right radicals. Indeed, a characteristic of many individuals involved in right-wing extremism is a culture of militarism and a fascination with weapons and explosives, and some far-right extremists have demonstrated intent and capability to acquire more sophisticated weapons and explosives, although, in fact, many individuals arrested with such materials had not undertaken any specific plot. Indeed, in the UK, the police arrested over 30 suspected right-wing extremists in July 2009 and seized as many as 300 weapons, including rocket launchers, pipe bombs and grenades from more than 20 properties in Yorkshire; there does not appear to have been an attack plot. Likewise, in 2006, two men were arrested in Lancashire for possessing large amounts of explosives; both held xenophobic views and had attended meetings organised by the British National Party but there was no developed plot. Groups or individuals arrested in the UK with more sophisticated weaponry, rather than homemade nail bombs or incendiary devices, are likely to have obtained these either through contacts with organised criminal groups or Protestant paramilitary groups in Northern Ireland, such as the Ulster Defence Association. Right-wing groups in the UK are also known to have attempted to recruit from the armed forces, theoretically giving better access to capability to launch attacks.

In Belgium, the police detained a group of 17 neo-Nazis in 2006 for plotting to stage attacks aimed at overthrowing the Belgian government. The group consisted of lower-ranking members of the Belgian Army, including non-commissioned officers, who were part of Blood and Honour, a neo-Nazi organisation originally founded in the UK but with members across Western Europe. Significantly, the group had obtained access to weapons and explosives, which was most likely arranged more easily through having members from the armed forces.

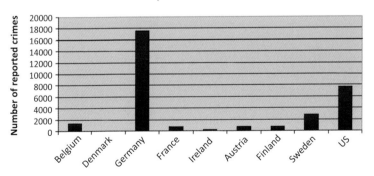

Officially recorded racist crime 2007

Source: European Union Agency for Fundamental Rights – Annual Report 2009; FBI Uniform Crime Report Hate Crime Statistics, 2007. This data relies on reported crimes by member states of the EU and FBI data; therefore, variance in reporting practices and criteria on what constitutes a 'racist crime' make a direct comparison between countries difficult.

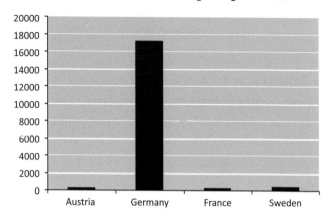

Recorded Crime with an Extremist Right-Wing Motive 2007

Source: European Union Agency for Fundamental Rights - Annual Report 2009

Right-wing Extremism in the US

A broad range of groups, including militia organisations and neo-Nazi groups, have seen a growth in their numbers even before the election of America's first black president, Barack Obama, the fact of which itself triggered vocal threats from extremist groups.

The Southern Poverty Law Center has estimated a 50% increase in the number of right-wing groups in the US between 2000-08. Ideologically, extremist groups in the US (such as the Christian Patriot Movement, White Aryan Resistance and Volksfront) have some ideological similarities to their Western European counterparts. However, far-right groups in the US are also preoccupied with the concern that the government (and especially a Democrat president and federal government) will infringe on their individual rights, such as the right to bear arms. In the bipartisan US system, far-right groups have effectively no political party presence, which means that individuals with these views are less easily co-opted into the political process.

The election of an African-American president has also led to a number of explicit threats and a few disrupted plots. According to investigative journalist Ronald Kessler, who interviewed Secret Service agents, President Obama receives an average of 30 death threats per day, a 400% increase on the figures for President Bush. In August 2008, the police arrested four individuals who they allege made racist comments and threatened to assassinate Barack Obama at the Democrat National Convention in Denver, Colorado. The police also seized a number of weapons. In October 2008, two men, who were active on white supremacist websites, were arrested on charges of plotting to assassinate Obama and to kill 88 African-American students in Tennessee.

As disaffection, over unemployment or the election of an African-American president for example, increases the appeal for some of right-wing extremist groups, we expect an increased frequency of bomb attacks and shootings against federal government buildings, courthouses and individuals and assets associated with minority religious and ethnic groups.

Currently, groups are capable of carrying out arson attacks, shootings and pipe bombings and, as in Western Europe they will target immigrants, Jews, Muslims and homosexuals and their property and businesses. Mosques, synagogues and black and Hispanic churches and schools are also preferred targets for right-wing extremists. We expect higher frequency in southern and Midwestern US, where right-wing extremists are most active and command greater support. Furthermore, a Department of Homeland Security report suggested that right-wing groups are likely to try to recruit disgruntled veterans, which would potentially increase their ability to plan and carry out attacks.

Acquiring large amounts of explosives is more difficult now than prior to the Oklahoma City bombing in 1995. Legislation governing the purchase and storage of explosive materials was tightened in the aftermath of the bombing and, at the time of writing, the Department of Homeland Security is working on the implementation of Section 563 of the FY08 Homeland Security Appropriations Act (Section 563 is called 'Secure Handling of Ammonium Nitrate'), which would make it more difficult to acquire large quantities of explosives ingredients by registering purchases and the identity of buyers. Despite these improvements, there are still regular incidents of small bombings and small explosives seizures across the US. Beyond this, there are instances of explosives theft from commercial operations. For example, in 2008, 150 pounds of blasting agent and 75 blasting cups were stolen from a container on a hillside in Blackstar Canyon, Cleveland National Forest, California, and in July 2009, 96 pounds of TNT belonging to the Washington State Patrol and 17 sticks of dynamite belonging to the Forest Service were stolen from storage at the Port of Walla Walla, Washington. Moreover, there have been cases of individuals and groups stockpiling large volumes of weapons and explosives, undetected, in some cases, for many years. For example, in July 2009, a sheriff was killed while trying to arrest a gunman with extreme right-wing views in Texas; the police later found a cache of more than 100 incendiary devices.

Descriptions of Selected Right-wing Groups in the US

Group	Base/Area of Operation	Known Attack Modes
American Front (anti-Semitic, anti-immigrant, anti-Communist)	Based in California	Arson
Aryan Nations (neo-Nazi, anti-Semitic)	Based in southern US, but also active in Ohio, Missouri, Idaho and California	Molotov cocktail attacks
Ku Klux Klan (racist, anti-immigrant)	Active mainly in southern US	Assault, protests / rallies
Volksfront (neo-Nazi)	Active mainly in western US	Assault/murder, vandalism

Source: Exclusive Analysis

Selected Right-wing Terrorism Attacks, Plots and Arrests

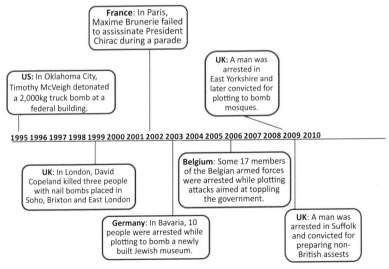

France: In Paris, Maxime Brunerie failed to assissinate President Chirac during a parade

UK: A man was arrested in East Yorkshire and later convicted for plotting to bomb mosques.

US: In Oklahoma City, Timothy McVeigh detonated a 2,000kg truck bomb at a federal building.

1995 1996 1997 1998 1999 2000 2001 2002 2003 2004 2005 2006 2007 2008 2009 2010

UK: In London, David Copeland killed three people with nail bombs placed in Soho, Brixton and East London

Belgium: Some 17 members of the Belgian armed forces were arrested while plotting attacks aimed at toppling the government.

Germany: In Bavaria, 10 people were arrested while plotting to bomb a newly built Jewish museum.

UK: A man was arrested in Suffolk and convicted for preparing non-British assests

Source: Exclusive Analysis

3. Russian Ports' Development: Strengthening the Commodity Supply Chain

For Russia, efficient and secure export of its raw materials is a strategic priority. Consequently, Russia is undertaking several large-scale port expansion programmes to increase its export capacity. This article highlights where port development is being prioritised given trade growth patterns, and examines several of the obstacles deterring foreign investment in the sector.

Russia's Ports

Source: Exclusive Analysis

Russia's ports are principally state controlled.

The Russian Ministry of Transport incorporated Rosmorport in 2003 to manage and develop port infrastructure on behalf of the state. On the federal level, Rosmorport cooperates with the Agency for Sea and River Transport, and the Ministry of Transport formulates its strategy. Rosmorport is financed through port duties that it collects for services. It owns port facilities and is in charge of their exploitation, modernisation etc., and is also the port operator.

Russia's Largest Ports

Port	Volumes (1H 2009)	Ownership
St. Petersburg (Morport)	- **5 million tonnes of cargoes;** a 5% year-on-year decline - export cargoes increased for steel (36%), coal (35%) and iron (13%)	JSC Sea Port of St. Petersburg: - Universal Cargo Logistics Holding B.V. (97%); purchased in late 2008
Novorossiisk	- **51 million tonnes;** an 8% year-on-year increase - handles 20% of Russian imports and exports	Novorossiisk Commercial Sea Port: -Russian Federation (20%); Kadina Ltd. (50.1%); Free-float (29.9%)
Arkhangelsk (Arseacoport)	- **0.7 million tonnes;** a 29% year-on-year decline	JSC Commercial Sea Port of Arkhangelsk; Norilsk Nickel (53%); Russian Federation (20%); Norilsk Gorni-Metalurgicheski Kombinat (19.7%)
Vanino	- **3.5 million tonnes;** an 88% year-on-year decline	Vanino Commercial Sea Port: Russian Federation (55%); Sistema; Monolit

Source: Exclusive Analysis

Investment Opportunities

New opportunities are likely to arise in Russia's eastern ports, particularly for grain and coal shipment.

Most Russian grain exports currently travel via southern ports, primarily Novorossiisk. However, in August 2009, it emerged that the Russian Grain Union was planning to increase exports to Asian countries in 2010-11, and that Russia was seeking investments by Japanese firms to build a grain terminal at one of Russia's Pacific ports. Russia's Far Eastern ports have already expanded in anticipation of rising Asian demand for coal. In 2008, for example, the Vostochnii port, located 150km southeast of Vladivostok, implemented a $10 million phase of its coal complex modernisation project.

Another phase of the project will see the construction of two 200,000-tonne capacity coal storage facilities. The main focus at eastern ports is on commodities, and container cargo facilities are being upgraded. In early 2009, Vladivostok took delivery of new cargo handling equipment, including four container handling cranes, which is likely to speed up operations at the facility. FESCO Transportation Group, for example, expects Vladivostok to increase its container throughput to 650,000 twenty-foot equivalent unit (TEU) in 2010, from 250,000 TEU in 2008.

Recent investments at Novorossiisk are likely to pay off in terms of higher oil and grain volumes, though the port is revising its growth targets due to the current economic climate.

Novorossiisk Commercial Seaport (NCSP) has been using funds raised in its 20% float in 2007 to implement extensive port improvements. Over 2007 and 2008, NCSP invested nearly $340 million in increasing cargo handling capacity. Already Russia's largest port, Novorossiisk saw a 10% rise in gross throughput during the first half of 2009, largely consisting of grains and oil. Although exports of Azeri oil via Novorossiisk declined following the opening of the Baku-Tbilisi-Ceyhan pipeline in 2006, total oil product shipments rose by 20% in the first half of 2009. That said, the port failed to meet its volume growth target in 2008, and in April 2009, NCSP placed its expansion plans under review given the subdued economic climate.

Western Russia's port capacities are increasing in terms of hydrocarbons shipping, but non-energy cargo projects are likely to be delayed given subdued economic activity.

In May 2009, Russian pipeline operator Transneft issued $1.1 billion worth of infrastructure bonds to fund construction of the Baltic Pipeline System-2

(BPS-2). The pipeline, with a projected annual capacity of 50-75 million tonnes, is scheduled for completion in 2012 and will carry crude oil from the Timan-Pechora basin in West Siberia to Russia's Ust-Luga port on the Baltic Sea. The first stage of the Baltic Pipeline System, completed in 2006 with a 75 million-tonne capacity, has already seen increased shipping volumes. Between January and May 2009, Russia's Baltic port of Primorsk, where the pipeline currently ends, saw a 3% increase in oil exports.

In August 2008, Russia's transport minister announced that Russia intended to stop using ports in the Baltic States for oil export by 2015, when the capacity of Ust-Luga is expected to reach 100 million tonnes per annum. At present, about 80 million tonnes of oil are transported through the Druzhba pipeline from southeastern Russia via Belarus and the Baltic States. By the end of 2009, Gunvor-controlled firm Rosneftebunker will have opened an oil terminal at Ust-Luga. Sibur Holding is building a liquefied hydrocarbon gas terminal (LNG and LPG), the first stage of which will become operational by 2011. In addition, container throughput at Ust-Luga has been growing steadily, up by 27% year-on-year in the first half of 2009 to 4.4 million tonnes. A second shipping channel is scheduled to be completed in 2010, at which point cargo capacity is forecast to reach 50 million tonnes.

However, global economic weakness has meant that some non-energy related construction projects at Ust-Luga have been put on hold. FESCO Transportation Group withdrew from the $800-million Ust-Luga Container Terminal project due to financing difficulties. FESCO claimed that there would be insufficient cargo to justify the Ust-Luga Container Terminal for at least the next three years, although this is contested by the terminal's UK investor, First Quantum. Also at Ust-Luga, Russian aluminium producer RusAl has temporarily suspended work on a $300-million aluminium loading terminal.

There is growth potential for Russia's northern ports due to recent tax changes and Russia's aim to stake its claim to Arctic resources.

In January 2009, Russian President Dmitry Medvedev passed new tax legislation, including a provision to eliminate certain taxes on fishing vessels which had led, for instance, to Murmansk-registered vessels being based in Norwegian ports. With the tax lifted, traffic through Russia's northern ports is expected to increase.

Moreover, as revealed in the Russian government's new 2009-20 national security strategy, Russia is keen to stake its claim to Arctic resources. Control over shipping routes is naturally a key component of this plan. It looks increasingly likely that a summer northeastern Arctic route between Europe and Asia, 4,000 nautical miles shorter than the equivalent southern route, will open within 10 years. An increase in oil, coal and metals exports from ports at Murmansk, Arkhangelsk and Dudinka is anticipated. In February 2009, Norilsk Nickel, which operates in the region, completed its purchase of a five-vessel Arctic fleet, and in March 2009 it opened a sales office in Shanghai, pointing to plans to increase exports.

In August 2009, German firm Beluga Shipping was the first non-Russian company to receive clearance to make the Arctic voyage from Vladivostok. Beluga Shipping had wanted to make the same journey during an ice-free period in 2008, but had failed to obtain the requisite permissions in time from the Russian government. As the government seems keen to exploit the economic potential of the passage, permission is likely to become easier to obtain, but as permission is still a requirement, it creates the risk of potential delays.

Obstacles to Russian Port Development

(i) The government's financial limitations.

The government, which is currently the major source of financing for port construction, has significant fiscal pressures. It is therefore concentrating funding on: developing facilities for the 2014 Winter Olympics in Sochi; developing transportation support networks for oil terminals, including those at the Eastern Siberia-Pacific Ocean pipeline (VSTO); and completing construction of the Ust-Luga port. Private investment has been relatively modest and limited mainly to institutional loans (see table below).

European Bank for Reconstruction and Development (EBRD) Investments in the Russian Port Sector

Project	EBRD Investment	Description
Development of System for the Operation of Shipping Transport (commenced 2005)	$7 million	Construction of port facilities and radio systems for the ports of Murmansk, Baltiisk and Kerch Straits. The $19-million project is intended to finance the construction of three radio towers and other supporting structures in Temriuk (Azov Sea), Kaliningrad (Baltic Sea) and Murmansk (Barents Sea). Rosmorport leads the project.
Regulatory Reforms (2007)	$96 million	A $150-million project for the promotion of tariff reform with regard to port dues, asset evaluation and changes in leasing arrangements of port infrastructure
Acquisition (2008)	$120 million	The EBRD purchased a 3.8% stake in FESCO to encourage the company's development of an integrated inter-modal transport system, as well as to improve corporate governance and environmental standards.

Source: Exclusive Analysis

(ii) Unclear regulatory frameworks and bureaucratic delays.

The Russian Ministry of Transport recognises the need to improve port structures and to use port facilities more effectively. However, it has not created a corresponding long-term strategy or the legal framework necessary to realise this development. Regulatory and bureaucratic impediments clearly discourage investors. For example, although a Concessions Law governing infrastructure development was passed in 2005, no concession agreements have been signed in the maritime sector. Concessions, if realised, would enable private operators to lease, develop or operate ports. In addition, laws governing public-private partnerships have yet to come into existence, but are essential to attract investment in ports. The EBRD-Rosmorport project to develop an operating system at the ports of Murmansk, Baltiisk and Kerch Straits was initiated in 2005, yet the requisite construction permissions have still not been obtained for the Baltiisk and Kerch Straits ports.

The Russian authorities have also expressed interest in setting up Special Economic Zones (SEZs) near port facilities. The aim is to create a favourable investment environment under a clear set of rules including tax exemptions and certain customs concessions. A law on SEZs came into force in 2007, including provisions for port SEZs, but thus far only three river ports have applied for SEZ status. Tellingly, the Ust-Luga port opted not to become an SEZ as the costs were judged to be too high (approximately €100 million) and the system of governance non-transparent. Indeed, overall interest in SEZs has been limited due to relatively modest tax concessions, minimum investment requirements and restrictions on resident companies' activities.

(iii) The politicised legal process and weak law enforcement.

State intervention risks are also considerable. The most telling example comes from the experience of Finnish subsidiary Moby Dick, which operates a container terminal at Kronstadt (St. Petersburg port). In 2006, the Russian authorities requested the return of some of its land and blocked access to the terminal, causing interruptions for foreign firms using the facilities. Eventually, Moby Dick's 49-year lease was revoked. FESCO was reportedly behind the attempted takeover. Overall, the port and shipping sector is dominated by Russian firms with strong establishment relations. This places foreign parties at significant risk of contract frustration and commercial disputes, as well as outright expropriation.

(iv) Organised criminal groups and corruption at Russian ports.

The problem of organised crime is most pronounced in the Far Eastern Russian ports, with criminal groups engaging in a wide range of smuggling activities. Most recently, for example, in July 2009, the police broke up a Russian organised criminal gang involved in importing contraband car tyres from Japan into the Russian port of Nakhodka. Local authorities are also known for illegal and corrupt activities. For example, former mayor of Vladivostok, Vladimir Nikolaev, was accused of bribery and illegal sales of city property. Corruption among customs officials often affects cargo transit through Russian ports, with authorities demanding bribes to process documentation. In 2007, for instance, a group of customs officers was arrested for requesting bribes to speed up document-processing times.

(v) Environmental protesters pose an increasing risk of disruption to cargo shipments.

Protests have already taken place at Russian ports, primarily with regard to oil and nuclear waste. One of the first such protest campaigns was led by the World Wide Fund for Nature (WWF) in 2005, when the government switched the construction of an oil terminal from the Vostochnii port to Perevoznaia Bay, which environmentalists claimed was more vulnerable to oil spills. After a two-year delay, it was eventually decided to move the terminal to Kozmino Bay. In 2008, the state environmental watchdog Rosprirodnadzor underlined a threat of oil pollution in the waters off Arkhangelsk, which has a potential to stimulate protests at the port. Demonstrations are also held in St. Petersburg against uranium waste arriving from Germany. The most recent protest was held in March 2009 by Russian groups Ecodefence, ECOperestroika and Greenpeace Russia, although such actions have thus far not involved direct action against the port facilities or vessels.

The three-year outlook

In summary, the risks to Russian port development and investment from excessive government control, the monopolistic dominance of domestic port and terminal operators, crime, bribery and commercial disputes are unlikely to diminish, at least in the three-year outlook. Port SEZs, which in theory offer protection to investors from many of these problems, are in the very early stages of implementation and will probably not become a significant factor in port development. Opportunities do exist, however, in areas that the Russian government is particularly keen to develop, such as the northern and eastern ports. China is likely to become a significant investor in Russia's eastern ports. For example, in a bilateral meeting in September 2009, Chinese officials agreed to cooperate in improving infrastructure at Russian ports near the Chinese border, partly due to the necessity of constructing a new terminal at Kozmino (near Nakhodka) for oil exports from the VSTO pipeline. Meanwhile, however, the slow pace of modernisation and capacity upgrades at Russian ports will hamper Russia's aspirations to establish itself as a major global economic power, for instance by limiting oil export capacity and causing delays to cargo delivery due to backlogs.

5. Latin America

1. Behind the Headlines: Violence in Mexico and Central America

President Calderón has stated that Mexico plans to invest over $230 billion in infrastructure, through private-sector partnerships. This plan will create opportunities for foreign and local businesses, especially in the oil and gas and construction sectors. This article examines the kidnap and murder risks to expatriate residents, visiting executives and staff, and civilians in Mexico and Central America. With inputs from EA's Executive Protection analysis, it asserts that the great majority of drug cartel violence in Mexico is targeted rather than indiscriminate and that, while kidnapping is increasing, foreigners are not the preferred target. Risks of violence to individuals are higher in some of Mexico's Central American neighbours to the south, especially Guatemala and Honduras.

The number of murders attributed to Mexico's drug cartels more than doubled in 2008 to around 6,000 and is on track to surpass this for 2009 at the time of writing.

Beheadings have become relatively commonplace, as have shootouts using high-powered assault rifles and grenades in urban areas. This has led to increasingly sensational media headlines about Mexico's 'drug war' and accusations that Mexico is becoming 'a failed state'. In addition to regular editorials of that nature in national US newspapers and regular reports in southern states' newspapers about cartel violence, a number of US government reports at the beginning of 2009 highlighted these concerns. The Joint Forces Command listed Mexico on a par with Pakistan in terms of risks of a 'rapid and sudden collapse'. Outgoing CIA Director Michael Hayden also included violence in Mexico on the same list of threats to US security as Iran's pursuit of nuclear weapons. Moreover, former US Homeland Security Chief

Michael Chertoff said that a 'surge' plan had been drawn up to deploy aircraft, armoured vehicles and military personnel to southern states, should civilian agencies there become overwhelmed by any spillover of violence from Mexico. Despite the deployment of 45,000 Mexican Army troops to support the police, there is unlikely to be a notable reduction in the levels of violence until clear winners emerge in relation to disputes over specific drug routes and trafficking hubs. Although the authorities are likely to arrest some senior cartel members in the next year, these tend to be replaced quickly. Furthermore, such transitions are often accompanied by an upturn in violence as pretenders position themselves to fill the power vacuum.

Trends since 2008 indicate that risks of cartel violence in Mexico are likely to be greatest over drug entry routes in Chihuahua, Baja California and Sinaloa; kidnapping tends to be most frequent in and around Mexico City.

The locations with the highest death tolls from the 'drug war' in 2008 were Chihuahua (mainly Ciudad Juárez, 36% of all fatalities), Baja California (mainly Tijuana and Mexicali, 12%) and Sinaloa (17%). These regions are likely to see the most intense violence through 2010 given the ongoing dispute between cartels for control over these key drug entry routes to the US. The Gulf cartel has split into two factions, respectively headed by Heriberto Lazcano (leader of Los Zetas, the group formed from former members of Mexican and Guatemalan special forces soldiers and policemen that formerly acted as the 'enforcement' arm of the cartel before becoming a cartel in its own right) and Eduardo Costilla. The Federation has also split into two main groups, one headed by Joaquín Guzmán (Sinaloa cartel) and Ismael Zambada (Pacífico), the other headed by Arturo Beltrán Leyva. The latter has struck an alliance with Lazcano, but there have been no reports of a countervailing alliance between Guzmán and Costilla. The Beltrán Leyva-Lazcano alliance is a particularly deadly combination, as Arturo Beltrán Leyva used to be in charge of the security of the Federation leaders and is thus in possession of

Concentration of kidnaps and drug cartel killings in Mexico

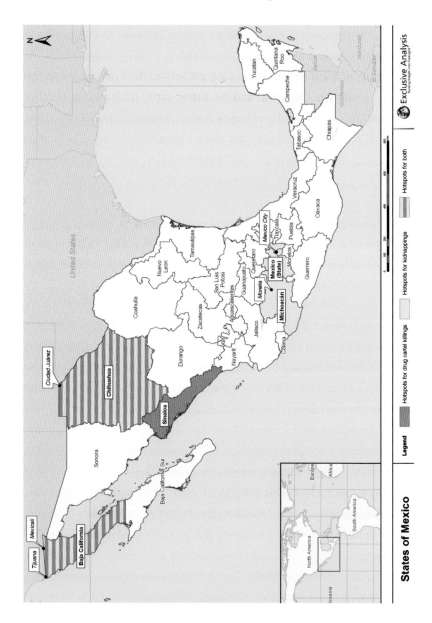

intelligence that makes them very vulnerable. The Beltrán Leyva organisation was also responsible for the most damaging top-level infiltrations of the federal law enforcement establishment. It must be noted that some of the second-tier cartels that had been written off as virtually disbanded due to the capture of many of their leaders are still active. This is the case with the Tijuana cartel (Baja California) and the Juárez cartel (Chihuahua). Another minor contender is the La Familia organisation (Michoacán). Although many kidnappings occur in areas which also have the highest homicide rates, they are far more dispersed countrywide. The kidnapping hotspots in 2008 were México state (16% of all reported cases), Mexico City (15%), Baja California (10%), Michoacán (5.5%) and Chihuahua (5.4%).

Around 90% of the victims of drug cartel violence have some degree of affiliation with a given cartel. Collateral killings or injuries of uninvolved civilians and damage to private property have been minimal.

There are some difficulties in assessing the historical data; specifically, it is very difficult to definitively confirm whether or not individual casualties were connected in any way with a cartel. However, there is some convergence around the conclusion that roughly 90% of victims are involved with the cartels. Police and military reports put the total number of fatalities on the government side in 2007-08 at roughly 7% of the total toll. Of these, about a fifth were members of the military and some were public prosecutors, but the majority were police officers (some of whom will have been killed because of their allegiances with a rival cartel rather than in operations against the cartels). Another report by a Mexican NGO, the Centro de Derechos Humanos Miguel Agustín Pro, lists 22 cases of innocent civilians being killed in 2007-08, or around 0.3% of the cartel-related killings in that period. The deaths of eight civilians after two grenades were thrown into a street party in Morelia, Michoacán, in September 2008 is a notable exception in terms of uninvolved civilians deliberately being targeted. In relation to visitors, projections of partial data from the US State Department suggest that approximately 40 US nationals were killed in Mexico in 2007-08. As US nationals account for more than 80% of all foreign visitors, we use these figures as a proxy for the risk to foreigners more generally. Of these homicides, 15 were classified by the US State Department as 'drug-related' or as 'executions', a term commonly used in Mexico to refer to killings by drug gangs. These figures will also involve incidents such as overdoses among users, killings by people the police believe were high on drugs, violent robberies by people seeking funds to buy drugs or drug purchases that end in violence.

Kidnapping rates have increased in Mexico, with incidents becoming more violent; expatriates and tourists are, however, unlikely to be targeted often.

Reported cases of kidnap-for-ransom (excluding 'express' and 'virtual' kidnappings) more than doubled from 476 in 2007 to 1,028 in 2008. Express kidnappings involve people being kidnapped off the street and forced to withdraw money from cash machines for the assailant's benefit. Virtual kidnappings take the form of assailants falsely claiming that an individual has been kidnapped (often this is done when verification is difficult, e.g. when the alleged victim's phone is turned off while they are on a plane or in the cinema). These types of kidnappings tend to be treated in the data as robberies rather than kidnap-for-ransom. Kidnapping for ransom is frequently a sideline of the gangs of gunmen acting as cartel 'enforcers' and corrupt police officers are often involved. It is also worth noting an increase in violence associated with abductions, including mutilations, rapes and executions of victims, even when a ransom has been paid.

Most of the victims are Mexican nationals, with the children of wealthy executives and those who work in sectors that handle large amounts of cash (e.g. food wholesaling) popular targets. In a July 2009 Public Security Ministry report (El secuestro: conceptos y estrategia de atención), it was reported that 28% of kidnapping victims they surveyed were 'shopkeepers and traders', 21% were 'students', 16% were 'employees' and another 15% were 'businessmen'. However, it is increasingly common for even relatively poor people to be kidnapped for ransoms of just a few hundred dollars. US authorities recorded just under 60 kidnappings of US nationals between 2006 and 2008; most of these took place close to the US-Mexico border, with Tijuana, Mexicali and Ciudad Juárez all kidnapping hotspots.

These statistics are, however, limited as it is very likely that the majority of kidnappings are not reported. NGOs that track these trends differ significantly in their collation methods and the size of samples used to then make nationwide assumptions. An NGO report from 2008 estimated that only one in seven kidnappings in Mexico is reported; another put this at one in 10. The most commonly used benchmark in recent years has been one in four. There are a number of reasons why a kidnapping would not be reported, including well-founded concerns that police officers are working with the kidnappers. Other cases are not reported because they may be related to disputes between criminals. However, the authorities claim that the statistical leap between 2007 and 2008 is largely attributable to the public's greater willingness to report kidnappings.

The current pattern of violence does not suggest that cartels are on the verge of mounting a major campaign to challenge the state as Pablo Escobar did in Colombia in the early 1990s.

In the late 1980s and early 1990s in Colombia, drug lord Pablo Escobar began detonating car bombs in public places and promised to pay $1,000 to any hitman who could prove he had killed a member of the security forces. Incidents included an 1,100lb truck bomb that destroyed the headquarters of the internal intelligence agency (killing 50), a bomb that downed an internal flight incorrectly suspected of carrying a presidential candidate (killing 110) and car bombs against several shopping malls, a bullring and newspaper offices. This was largely a reaction to the pressure brought by the US government under President Bush Sr, when top cartel leaders were extradited to the US and large seizures of cash and drugs were made. The turf war between the Medellín and Calí drug cartels in Colombia also included many car bombings against senior cartel members and buildings they owned.

Mexican drug cartels are not completely averse to the use of explosives. In February 2008, a small homemade bomb exploded prematurely as it was being prepared to be placed under the car of a senior policeman in one of Mexico City's busiest commercial and entertainment districts. In July 2008, authorities found two rudimentary car bombs made from gas canisters and petrol cans wired to cell phones stored in a safe house in Culiacán, Sinaloa – the first recorded example of this weapon being employed in Mexico. Then, in September 2008, two members of the La Familia cartel were arrested near Morelia, Michoacán, with six tubes of C4 explosives. Our sources report that the younger generation of cartel operatives are more willing to risk collateral victims in their attacks on rival cartels or representatives of the state. Under President Calderón, extraditions of drug traffickers to the US, along with drug and cash seizures (all factors that drove Escobar's bombing campaign in Colombia), have increased. Nevertheless, our view is that Mexico's cartels have yet to be put under the type of sustained and intense pressure that would lead them to cross the line and begin a bombing campaign in public places. It is noteworthy that there have been no major incidents involving the cartels and explosives since the significant public revulsion over the 2008 grenade attack on civilians in Morelia. That said, our sources report growing concerns within the Mexican security establishment over the possibility of targeted car bombs against senior officials. Such risks would increase if the cartels began to suffer significant and regular losses, for example due to a significant increase in the amount of US counter-narcotics efforts or at the hands of the new national police force. Neither of these scenarios is likely through 2011. Nevertheless, it is feasible that the cartels will increase bombing activity in public places ahead of mid 2012 presidential elections in order to intimidate the electorate and create an impression that the ruling PAN party's counter-narcotics strategy isn't working.

The Security Sector and Reform Efforts in Mexico

The Mérida Initiative: In October 2007, the US unveiled the Mérida Initiative to provide equipment, technical advice and training from 2008 to 2010 to confront organised crime in Mexico, Central America, the Dominican Republic and Haiti. Some $1.15 billion is earmarked for Mexico, which is, by one estimate, roughly 3% of what Mexico plans to spend on confronting the cartels. By mid 2009, Mexico had only received around $150 million. In contrast, Colombia has received around $6 billion in (mostly counter-narcotics) US aid since 1999.

Police Restructuring: There has long been a lack of coordination between the approximately 370,000 officers under myriad police forces. Up to early 2009, there were two federal forces with nationwide jurisdiction: the Federal Investigations Agency (AFI), under the Attorney General's Office, and the Federal Preventative Police (PFP), under the Public Security Ministry. There are also separate federal customs (PFF) and immigration (INM) bodies. President Calderón announced plans in 2008 to create a single federal force that would merge the responsibilities of these four federal entities. The 31 states, plus Mexico City, also have two forces each: a Preventative and a Judicial (investigative) force. Some of Mexico's 2,400+ municipalities have also opted to create Preventative and/or Judicial forces: some 1,650 forces in total. AFI (itself created in 2001 to replace the Judicial Police Force) was disbanded in May 2009 following the discovery of deep penetration by the cartels. It was replaced by the Federal Ministerial Police, staffed mainly by vetted and retrained AFI agents. By one estimate, up to 1,000 former AFI agents went to work for the cartels.

Customs: In August 2009, all 700 officers of the PFF customs body were replaced with 1,500 'foreign trade officers', who have undergone extensive training and vetting and are much better paid than their predecessors. In addition to manning US border crossings, they will address collusion with drug cartels at the port of Veracruz and Mexico City's main airport.

Army Deployments and Desertions: The number of troops in anti-cartel operations in 2009 fluctuated from 36,000 to 45,000, and the accompanying federal police contingent rose to 30,000. There is no date for troop withdrawal, but in September 2009 troops began to stand down from patrol in Ciudad Juárez. Around 10% (18,000 soldiers, including 40 special forces) of the Army deserts each year. It is estimated that a third go on to work with cartels.

Arrests and Operations: The government says that it has handled 1,070 reports of kidnappings, freed 970 hostages, arrested 1,449 suspected kidnappers and broken up 203 kidnapping gangs. From mid 2008 to mid 2009, the government arrested 70 regional bosses of the main cartels, more than three times than in the preceding 12-month period. Ten high-ranking officials, among them the federal anti-drugs 'czar', as well as some 200 public servants, were dismissed in this period and are being prosecuted for collusion with drug cartels.

Budgets and Legislation: Since the 'national agreement for security, justice and legality' was signed in August 2008, the national public security budget has been increased by 44% and the funds assigned to the states and municipalities by 15%. Congress has legislated for the confiscation of criminals' assets, tightening penal code provisions and a register of mobile phone users.

Central America

Central America's status as a drugs transit point and the internationalisation of Mexico's inter-cartel dispute has led to an increase in risks to personnel in the region.

Central American nations are used as transit points for narcotics en route from Colombia and other producers to the US. It is increasingly common for local proxies to be paid in drugs rather than just cash, which leads to violent disputes between local criminal gangs, such as the maras (the street gangs originally formed by Central American emigrants in the US and later established in their home countries as a result of US deportations), for control of domestic distribution. Furthermore, Mexico's powerful cartels now have a much more prominent presence in Central America as they seek to avoid the government crackdown back home. This leads to inter-cartel disputes over control of drug routes being replicated in neighbouring countries. In Mexico, the homicide rate is less than 11 per 100,000 population, after factoring in approximately 6,500 homicides per year since 2004 that are not related to drug cartels. The rates in El Salvador and Guatemala are more than four times this and in Honduras almost six times as high.

Table 1

Homicides			
Region Rank	Country	Homicides per 100,000 population, 2008	Total homicides, 2008	2007-08 change
1	Honduras	57.9	4,473	+25%
	Jamaica	56.6	1,611	+2%
	Venezuela	48.1	12,870	-1%
2	Guatemala	46.7	6,200	+8%
3	El Salvador	44.2	3,175	-9%
	South Africa	37.7	18,487	-5%
	Colombia	35.2	16,140	-42%
4	Panama	11	368	+50%
5	Mexico	10.8	12,130	+32%
6	Costa Rica	10.4	435	+25%
7	Nicaragua	8 (2007)	462 (2007)	-4% (2006-07)
	US	5.3	16,184	-4%
	UK	1.3	784	+3%

Graph 1

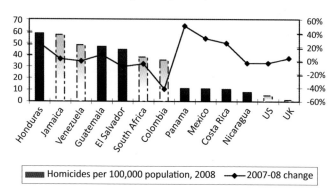

Homicides in Central America and Mexico
(plus Comparisons)

Table 2

		Kidnap		
Region Rank	Country	Kidnappings per 100,000 population, 2008	Total kidnappings, 2008	2007-08 change
1	Guatemala	1.6	213	+122%
2	Honduras	1	78	+86%
3	Mexico	0.9	1,028	+116%
4	Nicaragua	0.6 *(2007)*	34	-3%
5	Panama	0.4	13	+44%
6	El Salvador	0.2	13	-24%
7	Costa Rica	0.2 *(2007)*	7	+17% *(06-07)*

Graph 2

Kidnaps in Central America and Mexico

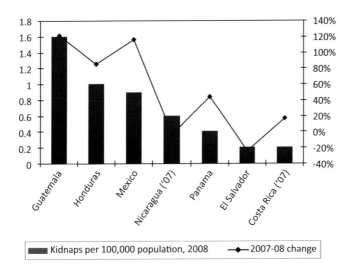

195

Sources for above Tables and Graphs: Announcements by government and police officials (systematic statistics, where they do exist, appear about two years late). The homicide figures are more reliable than those for kidnappings, as the latter are not always reported, out of fear for the lives of hostages or of security force involvement. Official figures only register reported kidnappings; NGOs tend to produce much higher figures based on assumed rates of under-reporting and the inclusion of estimates of 'express' kidnappings. Venezuelan data for 2008 is projected from nine-month total plus media reports.

In Guatemala, there has been extreme penetration of government structures, including the police and judiciary, by organised crime.

The faction of the Gulf cartel controlled by Los Zetas is particularly prominent in Guatemala. There have been several cases of the Mexican drug cartels' willingness to directly engage the Guatemalan state, for example by attempting to break arrested comrades out of prisons or mounting raids to steal military weapons. In March 2007, the UN High Commissioner for Human Rights, Anders Kompass, said that Guatemala was a 'failed and collapsed state'. Reasons cited have included the inability of security forces to dominate territory and the highest number of lynchings in Latin America. There has also been widespread killing of uncooperative candidates (those who may have refused to step down in order to allow the cartels to have their puppet candidate run unopposed or established politicians who refused an ultimatum/threat or bribe) ahead of elections in December 2008. Carlos Castresana from the UN's Commission against Impunity in Guatemala (CICIG) warned that 'Mexican drug cartels would run the country in two years' if action was not taken soon. The Guatemalan police believe that about 54% of all homicides are drug-related. Visitors, particularly tourists, have long been at risk of robbery, kidnapping and murder. In 2008, Guatemala had the highest kidnap rate in the region. Data for the first seven months of 2009 showed a 40% increase compared to the same period in

2008. The country's kidnapping hotspots are the departments of Guatemala, which includes the capital, Guatemala City, (32% of all reported cases in 2008), Suchitepéquez (23%) and Escuintla (18%).

The police and the judiciary have long been heavily involved in criminal activities and the 'parallel structures' that aid and abet organised crime in Guatemala. Discovery of these connections led to three replacements of the police's command structure in 2008-09. Furthermore, in early 2009, the public prosecution service initiated proceedings against 10 members of the police's anti-kidnap division accused of membership in, or collusion with, eight gangs of kidnappers operating in Guatemala City and the west of the country.

A key indicator going forward will be CICIG's success in mounting successful prosecutions in order to dismantle the infiltration of government agencies by organised criminal groups. Criminal gangs have been seeking to impede the CICIG by intimidating law enforcement and judicial officials with assassinations and threats. The growing reliance on the military to back up the police is likely to lead to a situation similar to that in Mexico. A central part of the peace accords at the end of the 1960-96 civil war was to cut the Army, which faced significant human rights abuse claims, from 45,000 to 15,000 soldiers. To compensate, the small police force expanded to 20,000 officers. However, this process was rushed through in just two years, leaving very little room for training or institution building. In parallel to an increase in the police force up to 30,000 by 2010, President Álvaro Colom is also seeking to increase the size of the Army to 25,000 by 2011. Nevertheless, many senior officers resent this role and we are aware of reports of patrolling soldiers simply seeking to avoid any potential trouble. Furthermore, some senior regional military commanders are thought to be major players in drug trafficking.

Homicides in Honduras, Costa Rica and Panama increased by 25-50% in 2008 and are unlikely to fall significantly in the coming years; however, the situation is improving in El Salvador.

Once at the top of the Central American murder league, El Salvador has seen its homicide totals fall steadily over recent years, most recently by 9% in 2008. An even greater decline has been recorded in the number of reported kidnappings: in 2007 they fell by 24% to 13, equivalent to a rate of 0.2 per 100,000 inhabitants, the second-lowest in Central America. Key factors there include improved policing and relatively less corruption, in particular reducing police collusion with organised criminal gangs.

Honduras, on the other hand, has among the highest per capita homicide rates in the world at 57.9 per 100,000, with a 25% increase from 2007-08; indeed, it is the highest among countries for which there is available data. Domestic violence is behind a large number of the homicides, and NGO workers and unionists are more vulnerable than politicians. There is no evidence that expatriates are, or are likely to become, major targets.

In Costa Rica and Panama, the number of homicides also increased significantly in 2008, by 25% and 50%, respectively, albeit it from much lower levels than Honduras. Panama's reported kidnappings rose by 44% and cases of armed robbery increased by 55% to 2,360.

2. Protests in Peru: The Outlook for Natural Resource Investors

Latin American governments have often taken for granted the passive compliance of indigenous communities to economic development projects on their ancestral lands. This article highlights Peruvian indigenous groups' major protests against the hydrocarbons sector in 2008-09. They led to the cancellation of four proposed laws and generated significant international attention when at least 34 people died in confrontations between the police and protesters. The article argues that such action is likely to embolden indigenous groups in the highlands to step up their own long-running opposition to mining (Peru is the world's largest producer of silver, third for copper, zinc and tin and fifth for gold). Partly motivated by these events in Peru, it is also likely that indigenous movements elsewhere in Latin America will step up their own protests in 2010 to restrict the development of oil, gas, mining, hydroelectric power, timber, agribusiness and other natural resource projects.

Indigenous groups in Peru's Amazonian regions have proven their ability to severely disrupt the country's oil and gas sector.

The Inter-Ethnic Association for the Development of the Peruvian Jungle (AIDESEP), an umbrella group of 57 organisations representing the 350,000 indigenous people from the Amazon lowlands in the north and east of the country, has brought an unprecedented level of coordination to its protest actions. It was able to mobilise simultaneously up to 30,000 people at sites hundreds of miles apart in August 2008 and then again in April-June 2009. The principal reason for these uprisings was a package of more than 30 laws that facilitate the development of natural resources in Peru's Amazon region. President Alan García bypassed Congress and issued these laws, which relate to stipulations in Peru's 2008 free-trade deal with the US, via presidential decree.

Disruptive unrest in Peru's Amazonian provinces (2008-09); oil, gas and aviation:

Date	Location	Incident
August 2008	Bagua, Amazonas	Protesters blocked a water supply canal to the El Muyo hydropower plant, cutting power in the region
	Cusco province	Argentine firm Pluspetrol was forced to halt operations at one of its Camisea gas fields due to an occupation by indigenous protesters
May 2009	Loreto province	State oil firm Petroperu was forced to halt the pumping of 27,000 bpd of oil through the Norperuano pipeline for around 10 weeks; daily losses were estimated at $120,000
	Napo river, Loreto	Several supply boats operated by Brazilian firm Petrobras were temporarily seized by protesters and other boats were prevented from reaching Block 67, operated by French firm Perenco
	Datam, Loreto	Protesters cut water and power supplies to Petroperu's Station No 5 oil facility
	Atalaya, Ucayali	Airport occupied for six weeks, disrupting commercial and cargo flights
	Cusco province	Protesters took over two valves of the Camisea gas pipeline until driven away by the police four days later
June 2009	Bagua, Amazonas	Some 24 policemen and at least 10 indigenous protesters died during confrontations
	Andahuaylas, Apurimac	Airport occupied for 13 days, disrupting commercial and cargo flights
	Trompeteros, Loreto	Airport occupied for a week, disrupting commercial and cargo flights
	Loreto province	Pluspetrol was forced to halt operations at its 1-AB oilfield due to protest actions

Source: Exclusive Analysis

Further disruptive protests against oil and gas assets are likely in Amazonas, Loreto, Cusco, Madre de Dios, Ucayali and Pasco until elections in April 2011, with the potential for more significant property damage than previously seen.

AIDESEP's protests led the government to delay a planned July 2009 auction of up to 20 new oil and gas exploration blocks in the Amazon. Furthermore, members of Congress from the governing APRA party sided with opposition legislators to repeal the four most contentious laws. In the face of strong international criticism over the 34 deaths in Bagua, Amazonas, in June 2009, the government also sought to restore order by reducing the length of leases and introducing more stringent social and environmental guarantees for natural resource companies. Nevertheless, the government has hardened its stance since then, pressing sedition and rebellion charges against AIDESEP leaders and announcing a new licensing round for 2010 as it pushes ahead with plans to double oil and gas output by 2014 from the current 143,000 bpd of oil and 327 million cubic feet per day of gas. As such, protests are likely to resurface periodically throughout 2010 and during the lead-up to April 2011 presidential elections. Potential triggers include government announcements of a back-track on the promises made in June 2009 to end the protests, or the imprisonment of AIDESEP members.

Future protest actions are unlikely to set out to cause property damage. Nevertheless, threats to set fire to occupied facilities in the wake of the Bagua deaths suggest that future incidents have the potential to cause more significant property damage than in 2008-09, especially if heavy-handed policing is employed. As before, the main targets are likely to be the country's most important hydrocarbons production and transport facilities in Amazonas, Loreto and Cusco. However, the combination of AIDESEP presence and oil and gas activity in Madre de Dios, Ucayali and Pasco also places these provinces at risk. Other companies operating in the Peruvian Amazon region include Repsol, Pan American Resources, Pacific Status Energy, Hunt Oil, Talisman Energy and Burlington Resources. The consortium operating the Camisea gas pipeline includes SK Energy, Sonatrach and Suez-Tractebel. The two-year construction of an extension to this pipeline (primarily by Peru's Kuntur and Brazil's Obebrecht) is due to begin in 2010 and is highly likely to be strongly opposed by indigenous groups and environmentalists more generally.

Mining Protests – the Central Highlands

Indigenous protesters have been active in the region for many years. For example, in June 2000, US firm Newmont saw its offices at Yanacocha, one of the world's largest gold mines, burned down following a mercury spill that poisoned hundreds. However, protest activity from these groups directed at mining operations is intensifying.

In part emboldened by AIDESEP's success, indigenous groups and local communities in the central highland regions are likely to step up their own long-running opposition to mining operations. Property damage is likely to be relatively minor, but has the potential to lead to business interruption.

Although several of the $17 billion worth of new mining projects planned for 2008-12 have been shelved due to the falling price of metals since mid 2008, many are still being developed in areas where local communities oppose the companies' presence, often due to pollution. Peru is the largest producer of silver, third for copper, zinc and tin and fifth for gold. According to the Public Ombudsman's Office, the number of social conflicts due to environmental issues rose by over 70% in the year to August 2009, to 135. Mining operations made up almost 70% of these, followed by oil and gas with around 10%. The most affected provinces are (in order): Cusco, Junín, Cajamarca, Ayacucho, Lima and Puno. The majority of Peru's mines are in mountainous areas. However, indigenous communities in the Amazon lowlands also oppose mining. For example, in January 2009, indigenous tribes in Huampani, Amazonas, kidnapped four workers from mining firm Afrodita for a week.

Incidents of unrest targeting mining assets

Date	Location	Incident
September 2007	Choropompa, Cajamarca	Villagers set fire to 10 hectares of land and damaged a water pipe at the Yanacocha gold mine
June 2008	Sandia, Puno	Some 500 local residents protesting over alleged pollution forced Peruvian mining firm Cartagena to abandon its Untuca gold mine for over five weeks; the site was looted
January 2009	Huampani, Amazonas	Indigenous tribes kidnapped four workers from mining firm Afrodita for a week
June 2009	Ituata, Puno	Two access bridges to the Mucumayo gold mine were blown up by protesters
	Orocampa, Ayacucho	Protesters blocked access to Buenaventura's Orocampa gold mine for two weeks
September 2009	Vista Alegre, Cajamarca	Some 1,500 locals opposed to a planned gold mine forced their way past 100 policemen into the camp and burned exploration equipment operated by Minera Consolidada
	San Marcos, Ancash	Two protesters attempting to break though the perimeter fence at Antamina, Peru's most productive silver mine, were wounded by police gunfire
	La Oroya, Junín	A policeman was killed by a rock thrown by those protesting over the potential closure of a metals smelter

Source: Exclusive Analysis

Property damage in anti-mining unrest tends to take the form of the burning of offices or equipment on the periphery of mine camps, or of vehicles either

Civil unrest against oil, gas and mining assets in Peru

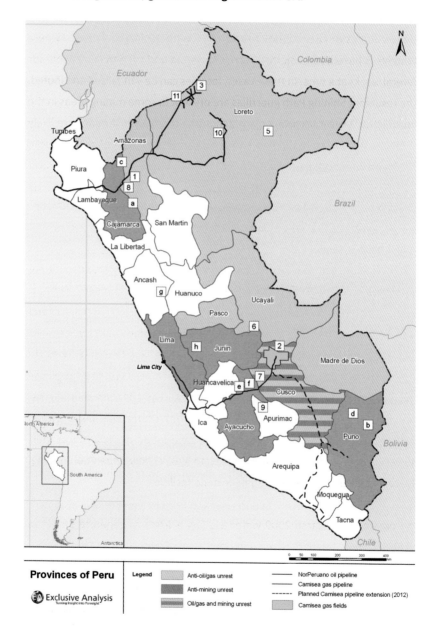

inside or close to the facilities. Security at mines producing significant amounts of metals tends to be fairly robust. However, this is not the case at smaller mines or camps that are still only in the exploration phase, where protesters have been able to overrun the sites and then occupy them for several weeks at a time. In these cases, facilities can be vandalised and looted. The resurgent Shining Path guerrillas are present in some mining areas in the south of the country. However, any actions by them against mines are likely to involve raids to steal supplies and dynamite. This was the case in October 2008 at a mine near Cobriza, Huancavelica, operated by Doe Run Peru. Specific mining projects facing unrest in 2010 include: Southern Copper's Tia María mine in Arequipa; Zijin's Rio Blanco mine in Piura and Gold Fields' Corona mine in Cajamarca.

Peruvian mines are also targets for often violent unrest by groups that are not necessarily opposed to mining operations. One of the most significant mining-related conflicts in 2008 was the dispute between Moquegua and Tacna provinces over the distribution of mining royalties paid by Southern Copper Corporation, whose operations straddle the two provinces. In addition to blocking the Pan-American Highway, protesters set fire to political party offices and ransacked other government buildings, including the tax agency. In October 2009, three people died during confrontations between rival groups of informal miners contesting the location of mine boundaries. However, given that most of these protesters ultimately depend on mining, they are unlikely to set out to damage mine facilities.

The passing of a March 2009 water use law is likely to generate unrest in 2010, which will impact on mining operations. Farmers claim that the law allows mining firms to siphon off water normally used for irrigation. In June 2009, the police drove back protesters who attempted to take over the airport in the tourist city of Cusco; they did, however, manage to blockade the rail line from Cusco to the Machu Picchu ruins. Farmers have threatened to escalate their protests in 2010, including direct action against mines. This is most likely in Puno and Arequipa.

Grass-roots indigenous groups throughout Latin America are becoming more politically dexterous, increasing the effectiveness and commercial impact of their protests against the development of natural resource projects.

Indigenous groups make up around 10% of Latin America's population of 500 million. Often assisted with funding and advice from international NGOs and organisations connected to the Catholic Church, indigenous activist groups are becoming increasingly adept at opposing what they perceive as encroachment onto their ancestral lands by domestic and multinational natural resource corporations. The increasing political influence exercised by indigenous groups across the region (exemplified by the December 2005 election of Evo Morales from the Aymara ethnic group as president of Bolivia) has resulted in an increasing amount of attention from mainstream media and political institutions to their grievances. Moreover, indigenous groups are increasingly working together with urban-based environmental groups with similar aims. Furthermore, it is likely that the socialist government of President Hugo Chávez in Venezuela, either directly or through allied governments such as Bolivia, will offer economic and other assistance to some of those opposing projects by Western multinationals. This would enhance their ability to organise protests and disrupt business activities. While there is no hard evidence of formal cooperation by indigenous groups across borders in organising specific protests, indigenous activism in one country is highly likely to have a powerful demonstration effect in neighbouring countries.

Regional hotspots for indigenous activism in 2010 are likely to include:

• **Ecuador**: Opposition to 2009 mining and water usage legislation has led the Shuars in southeastern provinces to mobilise. Mining operations in Azuay and Zamora-Chinchipe are likely targets, as is the planned initiation of oil exploration in Pastraza and Morona-Santiago. President Correa has taken a tougher line than his predecessors against incidents of unrest against key oilfields and pipelines in the northeastern states of Sucumbios, Orellana and Napo, which have periodically led to declarations of force majeure and major disruption to oil exports over the past five years. Nevertheless, local-level incidents of pollution or perceived broken promises of investment or job creation, are likely to spark isolated incidents of unrest in 2010. Road blockades around key facilities are most common, but the occupation (and minor vandalism) of pipeline pumping stations, local airports, vehicles and equipment is also likely, as are temporary kidnappings of staff (to force negotiations, not for ransom).

• **Chile**: The Mapuches in the southern Araucanía region are likely to step up their targeting of forestry firms and agribusinesses, as well as hydroelectric projects. Risks include arson and sabotage of farm vehicles, buildings and equipment, as well as the burning of cargo trucks.

• **Bolivia**: President Morales has raised expectations among the country's indigenous groups, which make up around a third of its nine million inhabitants, that they will enjoy greater rights over natural resource development. Hydrocarbons firms accused of failing to comply with new pro-indigenous laws risk having their concessions amended or taken back. Furthermore, impatience with the pace of reform is likely to see pro-government groups conduct violent land-grabs, affecting agribusinesses in the eastern lowland provinces of Santa Cruz, Beni, Pando and Tarija.

• **Central America**: Unrest tends to be smaller in scale and less violent than in South America but indigenous groups, especially in Panama, Guatemala and El Salvador, have proven themselves capable of successfully lobbying for the amendment or cancellation of mining and hydroelectric licences. Nevertheless, the global economic downturn means that governments are ultimately less likely to cave in to demands to cancel projects. This suggests that activist groups are more likely to begin adopting tactics such as kidnapping and sabotage of equipment.

3. Chávez's Vision: Workers Councils and Upcoming Nationalisations in Venezuela

After a decade in power, most indicators point to President Chávez accelerating towards his blueprint for a socialist economy: the Simon Bolivar Socialist Plan 2007-13. During the first half of 2009, Chávez extended state control over the domestic oil sector, took over a major bank and curbed the power of the media. This article examines the factors driving Venezuelan socialism and identifies which types of businesses are now at greatest risk of nationalisation. It charts the growth of Workers Councils and the impotence of political opposition.

The drivers of socialism, according to Chávez

In January 2007, shortly after Chávez's re-election, he described the five driving forces, or 'engines', for the construction of socialism in Venezuela:

- An enabling law (Ley Habilitante), already approved by Congress, which allowed Chávez to legislate by decree in 2007 and early 2008.

- Reform of the Constitution, approved in the February 2009 referendum, the most important element of which was removing term limits on the presidency.

- The infusion of 'moral guidance' into public institutions, a concept so far only vaguely developed.

- Reshaping Venezuela's territorial authorities (in progress). Chávez has already created regional military divisions that in early 2010 will overlap, and perhaps eventually supersede, state governorships. In this way, he has gradually removed powers from governors.

- Empowering people by creating Community Councils (a theme still being developed). Anecdotal evidence suggests that they are likely to have a significant say in many local matters including education, rubbish collection and the supply of water and electricity.

The clear and established trend of state takeover will continue.

In May 2009, the government seized the assets of about 70 local and foreign-owned oil service companies – gas injection plants, vessels and other assets – most of which were in the Lake Maracaibo region. These were taken over on the grounds that they were charging excessive rates for an essential service to the state-owned oil company Petroleos de Venezuela (PDVSA). The takeover happened just hours after the Venezuelan legislature passed a law authorising the government to take over operations by decree. The rapidity of the move could well set a precedent for the future. Ideologically, it was in line with Chávez's belief that Venezuela must promote endogenous growth. This means that wherever possible, services and other goods must be produced domestically either by state enterprises or collectively owned economic units.

Perhaps the other most important takeover in 2009 was the July 2009 government purchase of Banco de Venezuela, owned by Spain's Santander Group and Venezuela's third-largest bank. Chávez agreed to pay $1.05 billion in compensation to the Santander Group. The government also now owns Banco Industrial De Venezuela (BIV), having stepped-in in May 2009 when the institution was in financial distress. The BIV is now likely to be merged with Banco de Venezuela to form a large banking network. This banking network will be able to facilitate a range of government payments such as pensions, funding of public enterprises and allocation of subsidised credits to farmers and other social groups that the government favours. The risk of further takeovers in the banking sector in the near future has probably receded somewhat, now that the state owns 25% of the sector, which it uses to force private banks to adhere to lending policies promoted by the state.

Chávez is creating a legal framework to allow takeovers in multiple sectors.

Chávez's drive to extend his socialist policies in 2010 will be backed by the passage of several laws designed to strengthen state and worker control over many aspects of economic life. These laws will cover the themes of Social Property, Public Planning and Labour and so-called Workers Councils. In essence, these incoming laws will allow Chávez to declare any asset of social interest, and in turn allow it to be expropriated. The remit of the laws will facilitate the government's ability to take over and convert to 'social property' whichever business or asset it deems appropriate.

Given the vagueness of laws, potential targets are unclear. However, those most at risk are likely to be food processors and food distributors, petrochemical companies, large rural estates and hotels.

Food Companies
Food security is a highly sensitive issue for the government. Indeed, Chávez's loss of the December 2007 referendum was in part due to increasing food shortages in the months prior to the vote. In response, the government has sought to tighten control over food production as well as distribution. According to the Ministry of Agriculture, in four years time the state is expected to produce 25% of the country's food and control 30% of the food distribution network. The government has already taken steps in that direction. In early 2009, Chávez ordered the takeover of a Cargill rice plant on the grounds that it was violating a food security law. Also, two plants owned by Venezuela's Polar, the country's largest private company, were taken over. Food distribution companies are likely to be targeted, because the government has accused them of hoarding goods or 'speculating' with prices to the detriment of consumers. Food companies that are likely to be heavily fined, if not nationalised, include Excelsior Gama, Cargill, Polar Alimentos, Nestlé de Venezuela, Pepsi and Distribuidora Finefoods.

Petrochemical Companies

Petrochemical companies are likely to be affected, since the Chávez government considers them part of a strategic sector. State takeover of the petrochemical sector is seen by Chávez as the natural progression of oil nationalisation. He has long argued for Venezuela to diversify away from merely extracting oil. Companies that are most at risk include Industrias Venoco, Polinter and Tyco Group.

Rural Estates

The Land Institute, INTI, has vowed to make Venezuela free of *Latifundio* (large rural estates) by 2020. Since Chávez's arrival in office, the government has claimed 2.4 million hectares of land deemed idle (250,000 hectares in 2009). According to INTI, at least six million hectares can be considered *Latifundio*.

Hotels

President Chavez has also singled out hotels as a sector requiring more state participation. In October 2009, the government issued a decree authorising the takeover of the Hilton Hotel and Suite Complex on Margarita Island. The takeover was justified on the grounds that there is an 'urgent' need to develop the social aspect of the tourism industry in Nueva Esparta, the state to which Margarita Island belongs. The decree notes that the state will prioritise the development of 'sustainable tourism' in Nueva Esparta, namely that the industry's main goal should be to benefit local communities. This suggests that more hotel seizures in Nueva Esparta are increasingly likely. There is a precedent to this. In 2007, the Hilton Caracas Hotel was taken over and renamed Alba Hotel, after the name of the regional trade pact grouping Venezuela and other left-wing regional governments.

Some industries, such as energy, may be able to establish workable joint venture relationships, given Venezuela's need for technology and expertise that PDVSA lacks.

In September 2009, for example, Repsol-YPF said it had discovered as much as eight trillion cubic feet of offshore natural gas. In response, Chávez praised the find and pledged that PDVSA would work to develop the gas field on a 50-50 basis with Repsol-YPF. The findings are very preliminary as reserves need to be confirmed by independent parties and final contractual terms are still to be agreed. However, Chávez's initial stance points to a continued role in Venezuela for foreign energy multinationals. Some new Venezuelan businesses, notably some banks and food distributors, are owned by individuals who have emerged as a new wealthy elite over the past five years. They are likely to escape government intervention or nationalisation because the owners are close to Chávez.

Colombian assets face a heightened risk of nationalisation.

Chávez is displeased with Colombia's decision to allow US military bases on Venezuela's doorstep. He is responding on the trade front, diversifying away from Colombian suppliers in favour of those from other countries. Such action increases the risk that some Colombian assets will be nationalised in Venezuela, or that Colombian companies will see their operating licences terminated. Colombian firms with large subsidiaries in Venezuela such as food producer Alpina, chocolate maker Compania Nacional de Chocolates and retailer Exito, are at particular risk of being nationalised. Colombian cement maker Argos was nationalised in 2008 with no compensation yet paid.

Chávez's favourite inward investors are determined by their country of origin and type of company. Right now Russian, Iranian, Chinese, Brazilian and Spanish companies appear to be enjoying special treatment. In addition,

Chávez is more comfortable discussing investment deals on a government-to-government basis, and therefore favours state-owned companies from these countries.

Workers Councils are likely to see an increasing role in the economy.

President Chávez has been eagerly promoting Workers Councils, a kind of workers' cooperative, as one of the key pillars of Venezuelan socialism. This has been gaining prominence over recent years, but as Chávez steps up his revolutionary zeal it is highly likely that these grass roots organisations will gain an increasing role in economic management. Some companies in Venezuela have already been taken over by Workers Councils. In most cases, the targets are factories that have previously gone bankrupt, rather than companies that have been nationalised. In May 2009, for example, the government handed over sardine processor Conservas Alimenticias La Gaviota to a Workers Council, after the processing plant had been idle for two months. The government asserts that such takeovers are at the vanguard of Venezuela's economic transformation and are an integral part of the roadmap from capitalism to socialism.

There are not many success stories to highlight for companies whose assets have been fully transferred to a Workers Council. Many similar cooperatives that the government has established in the last five years, such as small textile producers, have failed. While bankrupt factories that are handed over to a Workers Council may have the advantage of physical assets such as machinery, and a capital injection from a state bank, they face the same problems in terms of marketing and production that led to the privately owned company's failure. Overall, this initiative has created employment or saved jobs, but the sustainability of these entities is questionable given the focus on worker benefit over cost-controlled productivity.

In parallel to the Workers Councils are Community Councils – civil organisations that are in theory autonomous and designed to increase local participation in the execution of public policy. However, in practice many receive some funding from the Chávez government. Community Councils could in some areas eventually operate in parallel with Workers Councils, although this is still probably several years off.

The southeastern region of Guayana will act as a pilot programme for Chávez's socialist plan.

Over the coming year, how relations develop between the government, worker groups and companies in the region of Guayana may well provide pointers to both policy choices and labour relations elsewhere in Venezuela. Chávez has suggested that the workers' movement in Guayana is instrumental to the foundation of socialism in Venezuela and will play a fundamental role in Chávez's Guayana Socialist Plan 2019. The still as-yet unfinalised plan aims to overhaul the heavy industries sector centred on Ciudad Guayana, such as loss-making aluminium producers, which have long been dogged by labour unrest. However, only a handful of the unions in the Guayana region are pro-Chávez, so civil unrest is likely in 2010. The main rationale behind the Guayana pilot programme is to give workers increasing decision-making in state-owned enterprises.

Reduced oil revenue is likely to depress compensation paid for takeovers.

Lower oil prices in 2009 compared to 2008 and reduced oil output have put considerable pressure on the Venezuelan government's finances. This means that even if Venezuela does compensate former owners of assets it plans to take over in the coming months, it is likely to do so both at rates below book value and by offering bonds, rather than cash. Venezuela still owes about $10 billion to companies for earlier nationalisations, and so a number of upcoming nationalisations will probably not be settled amicably, resulting in a series of new international arbitration cases involving Venezuela. Given the weakness of the economy and large public spending commitments, the $20 billion the government plans to raise through debt issuance is likely to be swallowed up quite fast.

The opposition poses little threat to Chávez, who is expected to stay in office until the 2012 elections.

Although food shortages, high inflation, authoritarianism and increasing criminality have somewhat dented Chávez's popularity, his position seems secure at least through to the next election in 2012. Chávez passed the test of a dramatic collapse in the oil price and he remains strong politically. At the time of writing, the oil price has recovered to about $75 per barrel and oil production deals with Russia and China are expected to bring $36 billion of investment in the next few years. At the same time, the eagerly awaited tender of the Orinoco Belt's Carabobo block is likely to occur in 2010. This is expected to attract sizeable investment from Western oil companies, eventually reversing Venezuela's decline in oil production.

A serious challenge from the opposition in the run-up to the election seems very unlikely. Chávez has significantly weakened and politicised most institutions. Over the coming year, the Chávez government will continue to disrupt pockets of opposition power, such as regional governors and local mayors and independent or opposition-aligned media entities. Also, while there is little room for dissent, the opposition itself remains highly disorganised without a credible agenda. It also lacks a leader with mass appeal capable of unifying its disparate factions, or appealing to the poor masses of Venezuelans, as Chávez does.

Map of Chavista governorships in Venezuela

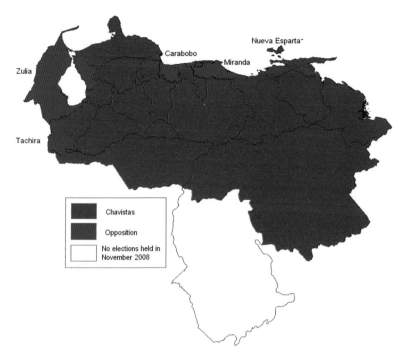

Source: Exclusive Analysis

March 2009 – Congress authorises central government to take control of airports and seaports; this deprives governors of key revenue
May 2009 – Congress removes 96% of the budget of the mayor of Caracas after losing the post to the opposition
September 2009 – President Chávez creates six new vice presidencies. Vice presidents are expected to oversee governors

6. Middle East and Northern Africa

1. Reintegrating Radicals: Comparing Results in Egypt, Saudi Arabia and Yemen

Governments engaged in domestic counterterrorism operations against militants, or whose nationals engage in violence abroad, face the problem of how to prevent extremists among the prison population from radicalising others, or from posing continued terrorism risks on their release. In the last few years, states have started to experiment with programmes attempting the reintegration and re-education of such individuals and to consider how such de-radicalisation programmes might support existing counterterrorism operations. There is no universal formula; the key factors determining the success of these programmes are the local conditions and culture of the host country. It is with Exclusive Analysis' specialist knowledge and local network that we are in a position to understand these conditions, and here we look at three de-radicalisation programmes and evaluate their success: Egypt, which runs one of the region's longest-established programmes; Saudi Arabia, whose Munasaha (Advisory Committee) is arguably the most comprehensive and best-funded, and Yemen, whose Religious Dialogue Committee was discontinued in 2005 after increasing evidence of its ineffectiveness.

De-radicalisation can generally be understood as a government-managed process that seeks to persuade militants to desist from violent jihad and to rehabilitate them in society. The process most often takes place in prison because of the ease with which detainees can be isolated from external influences and compelled to participate in the programme. From our observations, de-radicalisation is most likely to be successful when it takes a culturally specific approach tailored to the nature of the society into which an individual is to be released, the nature of the network to which they belong, and the origins of their radicalisation. Leveraging other social or government institutions (such as security agencies and family) to help ensure continued good behaviour on release also appears vital.

Although Yemen's de-radicalisation programme from 2002-05 required graduates to pledge political allegiance to the secular government, in Egypt and Saudi Arabia de-radicalisation goals have focused solely on renouncing violence and not on changing politically controversial views. There has been no attempt in Egypt, for example, to de-radicalise detainees from the non-violent Muslim Brotherhood opposition movement. Sources who have engaged with 'de-radicalised' individuals in Saudi Arabia confirm that most still uphold radical views, but do not act on them. Clerics in Saudi Arabia, for example, simply seek to convince detainees that the decision on the time and place of jihad is not up to the individual, and that only the Muslim head of state has the authority to declare jihad – the wali al-amr principle.

Even in the secular states of Egypt and Yemen, debates take place in an Islamic framework rather than by reference to secular law or any other concepts of morality. In Yemen, detainees in the 2002-05 programme participated in one-to-one discussions with Islamic legal experts, while Egyptian clerics use arguments based on the Islamic theory of fiqh al-maqasid (jurisprudence of objectives), emphasising the need for jihad to bring collective benefits to Muslims. In the words of recanted Egyptian Islamic Jihad (EIJ) leader Sayyid Imam al-Sharif, 'The enemy must be fought. But why kill the enemy's soldiers if [in response] the enemy may flatten your country?'

What criteria do governments employ for selecting individuals for de-radicalisation?

In Saudi Arabia and Yemen, individuals involved in domestic terrorism are not eligible for de-radicalisation.

The Saudi and Yemeni decisions not to de-radicalise and release those implicated in domestic terrorism (rather than low-level militants who have not staged attacks but who are sympathetic to al-Qaeda's ideas) is in large part due to the controversy that such a move would create, as well as the violent risk posed by such detainees on their release. By contrast, in Egypt, leaders have been less of a cornerstone of the Saudi and Yemeni de-radicalisation programmes. Clerics and operational leaders are influential, but the trends of transnational jihad and self-radicalisation undermine the value that co-opting a single leader would have in a more hierarchical structure (such as that offered by Egyptian jihadist groups in the 1990s). However, individual volunteer fighters abroad in places like Iraq or Chechnya are considered less 'radicalised' than those who engage in domestic terrorism, in part because the state considers them to be less of a direct threat. They are often targeted for de-radicalisation upon their return, however. Low-level jihadists represent the bulk of the 364 detainees released under Yemen's programme, and the 3,000 detainees selected for the Saudi programme.

In Saudi Arabia, an individual's pathway to radicalisation helps determine selection for a particular targeted programme.

Radicalisation patterns in Saudi Arabia indicate the importance of kinship, where individuals may be radicalised by a family member, or even through online interaction with like-minded individuals. For such detainees, an individualised, rather than a top-down, de-radicalisation approach has proved more successful. The Saudi programme determines the proportion of religious re-education and social and material incentives to be used on a case-by-case basis, depending on the pathway by which an individual was originally radicalised. For example, someone with a tendency towards criminality or risk-taking may be offered financial assistance to get married, in order to 'settle' him in society and give him responsibilities. Those with stronger religious convictions are likely to respond better to the theological element of the programme.

Targeting the leadership of groups is likely to be more successful in hierarchical terrorist organisations like the EIJ and Islamic Group (IG), where collective de-radicalisation can therefore be achieved.

In contrast to Yemen and Saudi Arabia, Egypt has focused on precisely those individuals whom it deems to pose the greatest internal security threat, namely senior leaders within EIJ and IG, both groups that engaged in a violent terrorist campaign in Egypt in the 1990s. Egypt has avoided the problem of controversial releases of senior jihadists who recant by keeping them in detention, so that they can be deployed for public communications and statements under tightly controlled conditions.

Egypt's de-radicalisation process began as a ceasefire declared by IG in July 1997. The Egyptian government initially failed to recognise the ceasefire and continued its repressive treatment of militant detainees until the Luxor massacre of foreign tourists in November 1997, after which the government decided to change its approach and allowed interaction with the IG to evolve. It facilitated meetings, lectures, discussions and various types of domestic and international communications between the leadership of the IG, its middle ranks and grass roots and then provided select inducements (release from prison, financial compensations, pensions, etc.) for de-radicalised members. Members of the IG who accepted the 1997 ceasefire and subsequent peace initiatives were eligible for the programme, as were members of al-Jihad who accepted a 2007 refutation of violent jihad written by EIJ leader Sayyid Imam al-Sharif. While recidivism figures are not published, Egypt claims that no released detainees have reoffended.

Who leads a de-radicalisation programme?

The Islamic community itself has the most credible intellectual tools to target beliefs and ideologies.

An important plank of de-radicalisation in all three countries has been detainee participation in religious discussions led by clerics in order to convince them of the illegitimacy of their actions. However, the clear danger for clerics is that their de-radicalisation efforts may be discredited with charges of torture or compulsion by state authorities. Al-Qaeda deputy leader Ayman al-Zawahiri responded to EIJ leader al-Sharif's attack on al-Qaeda with a jibe that the fax machine used to send Sharif's recantation ran off the same circuit as the prison's electrodes and torture equipment. Therefore, Egypt and Saudi Arabia have attempted to use clerics with well-established reputations outside the de-radicalisation context – in Egypt, using clerics from the world-renowned al-Azhar University, and in Saudi Arabia, through the influential Wahhabi clerical establishment. One difficulty is that even institutions like al-Azhar are often criticised by jihadists as subservient to the Egyptian government. Egyptian militants have shown themselves far more likely to listen to reformed clerics within their own organisation. In Yemen, the programme was controlled by moderate clerics aligned with the Muslim Brotherhood (distrusted by violent jihadists), compounding the credibility issue.

Other reformed or reforming militants are also a powerful tool, while the setting is also important.

Egypt pioneered the use of fellow prisoners, specifically credible leaders and clerics, to argue against radical views. Saudi Arabia holds its theological conversion efforts in classroom settings which allow discussion and questioning, while its Ministry of Islamic Affairs' Serenity chatroom lets clerics and participants work through dialogue online. In Egypt, interaction with reformed members of the IG helped facilitate the de-radicalisation process of the EIJ. Several Islamist leaders have argued that without the IG's de-radicalisation process, there would not have been an EIJ one. This suggests a 'domino effect' is possible between different groups operating in a similar context.

The Saudi Arabian programme includes communities and families in the de-radicalisation process.

The Saudi programme engages families in a dialogue process and, more coercively, forces heads of households to sign declarations of responsibility for the individuals undergoing the programme. Pressure on families is likely to consist of a combination of threatened social stigma, withdrawal of patronage and possibly threat of imprisonment to family members. Saudi authorities have frequently allowed convicts to obtain day release for events such as family funerals, on the condition that three family members guarantee their good behaviour. To date, no detainee on day release has absconded, and at least two militants released from the programme who rejoined al-Qaeda in Yemen have now handed themselves back in, due to family pressure. Fawaz al-Utaibi handed himself in to Saudi authorities in September 2009 after reported negotiations with his family, while Saleh al-Awfi, who escaped to Yemen and appeared in a jihadist video in January 2009, handed himself in after Deputy Interior Minister Prince Muhammad bin Nayef, who founded and heads the Kingdom's de-radicalisation programme, made a personal visit to his family to engage their cooperation in securing his return. In fact, al-Qaeda in the Arabian Peninsula (AQAP) justified its subsequent assassination attempt against Prince Muhammad in a statement referring to the Prince's unacceptable use of pressure on militants' wives and families.

What makes for success/failure in de-radicalisation?

Collective de-radicalisation is more likely to be successful in traditional hierarchical groups, but these are less and less common in today's jihadist organisations.

Of the three countries examined in our case studies, Egypt Is the only one which has successfully implemented collective de-radicalisation. Four factors are usually at play in successful collective de-radicalisation:

- the co-opting of an influential leadership
- physical disruption by the state to the point where a group can no longer actively function
- multi-party interactions not controlled by the state (where jihadists engage with other non-violent ideologies)
- selective inducements from the state and other actors

The absence of any of these factors may contribute to re-radicalisation (for example, weak leadership results in factionalism, which in turn reduces internal pressure on individuals to recant).

In Egypt, powers granted to security services meant that the state was able to disrupt the EIJ and IG's terrorist networks, holding suspects without charge for long periods to ensure that the group could no longer function properly. In countries where intelligence agencies have less far-reaching powers, active disruption can be problematic since sufficient evidence must be gathered to successfully charge and convict each member, while the growing trend of small self-radicalising cells makes top-down de-radicalisation difficult. Success was also in large part due to the IG's cohesiveness, since the group was formally structured and highly insular. Yet, in most cases today, Islamist groups have abandoned this type of rigid hierarchy and there is frequent disagreement, even with founding ideologues and leaders, making the Egyptian model difficult to apply elsewhere.

Co-opting radicals through social and economic incentives is likely to be problematic outside a patrimonial culture.

The Saudi approach to radicalisation reflects specific characteristics of the Arabian peninsula's culture, where rulers are expected (and financially able) to provide materially for their people, and where dissenters are often co-opted rather than confronted. One key difficulty with the use of social pressure to ensure cooperation is that such tactics only work where extended family networks are present in the country. One Saudi militant based in Yemen, Said al-Shihri, brought his wife and children over to Yemen in May 2009, probably to avoid them being used against him.

In Egypt and Yemen, economic constraints make effective aftercare and engagement by the state more problematic.

Material incentives offered by the Saudi state which help ensure continued good behaviour are difficult to replicate in less wealthy states. In Egypt, a powerful security apparatus helps keep track of militants released from prison, which mitigates the state's inability to offer incentives on the Saudi scale. However, in Yemen economic constraints are coupled with a lack of capability on the part of security services to maintain follow-up surveillance, which increases the chances of recidivism.

In Yemen, failure or inability to broaden participation outside the state's political security and apparatus contributed to the programme's ultimate failure.

While the current Saudi programme places a great deal of emphasis on securing the cooperation of detainees' families, during Yemen's de-radicalisation programme from 2002 to 2005 detainees' families were frequently unaware of where they were being held. There was no attempt to co-opt families at the start of the process. While tribes were asked to take responsibility for detainees' good behaviour on their release, the fact that some tribes actively combat the state meant this was a difficult mechanism to rely on.

Significantly, one of the reasons for the Yemeni programme's failure appears to have been an insistence on too many goals.

Yemen's de-radicalisation programme from 2002-05 required graduates to sign up to the rejection of violence, respect for non-Muslims, and – most problematic of all in Yemen – the acceptance of the Yemeni state under Islamic law. Yet, this is arguably superfluous to any de-radicalisation goal – many in Yemen's political opposition movements deny the state's authority and are not deemed criminal. The programme was also compromised by the state's willingness – according to detainees' reports – to waive legal rights, use torture and bully detainees. This necessarily undermined the programme's credibility and increased the likelihood that detainees would become more, not less, radicalised during their time in prison.

What impact does de-radicalisation have on terrorism risks?

In Egypt, hierarchical terrorist groups have given way to self-radicalising cells, which are less capable but are also less susceptible to collective de-radicalisation.

In Egypt, there has not been a terrorist attack by either the EIJ or IG since the 1997 Luxor massacre. Admittedly, the primary reason for this is likely to be the large-scale arrest sweeps and prolonged detentions that followed this incident. Another is that the EIJ and IG had in any case lost much of their popular support due to a series of attacks on civilian and tourist targets that also damaged the livelihoods of Egyptians earning a living from tourism. Nevertheless, had the major leaders not renounced violence from within prison, we would have expected to see at least some small-scale revenge attacks by supporters on the outside. It appears that in Egypt, a combination of de-radicalisation of key leaders, intense pressure by security forces and public weariness of the sustained terrorist campaign all contributed to defusing the threat formerly posed by the EIJ and IG.

Despite Egyptian successes against the EIJ and IG, it is less clear whether the recantations of leaders such as Sayyid Imam al-Sharif are easily transferable for use in de-radicalising others, especially outside Egypt, where many jihadists will not even have heard of the EIJ and IG except perhaps through al-Qaeda leader Zawahiri's own well-publicised criticisms of those groups. In Egypt itself, since al-Sharif recanted in 2007, there have been a number of small-scale terrorist incidents (most recently a bomb in the Khan al-Khalili market in February 2009) by a younger generation of self-radicalising jihadists for whom decisions by the EIJ and IG are likely to have little significance. It is unlikely that Egypt will succeed in implementing the same de-radicalisation strategy with this newer generation, who will require a more individualised approach.

Saudi Arabia's successful combination of counterterrorism offensives and de-radicalisation strategy has been undermined by the potential for released detainees to abscond to Yemen.

In Saudi Arabia, there have been more cases of released detainees rejoining terrorist groups, attempting to travel to destinations where there is a jihadist infrastructure to rejoin like Pakistan, or simply re-contacting fellow jihadist sympathisers. One significant problem is the ease with which released detainees can cross the border into Yemen, where a number of other Saudis wanted by authorities continue to pose a terrorism threat to Saudi Arabia. Indeed, though a combination of de-radicalisation and counterterrorism offensives by the security forces have significantly reduced terrorism risks in Saudi Arabia, a number of incidents this year indicate that attacks are now most likely to be directed from Yemen. As noted, however, family pressure can help guard against Saudi militants absconding to Yemen, and the state claims around an 80% success rate to date for its de-radicalisation programme.

The effectiveness of the de-radicalisation programme in reducing the pool of support for jihadist terrorism can be measured by the extent of opposition to it among those jihadist leaders still at large. It is noteworthy that AQAP attempted in August 2009 to assassinate the founder and figurehead of the de-radicalisation programme, Prince Muhammad bin Nayef. Nevertheless the prevalence of conservative Wahhabi Islam in Saudi Arabia, and generally widespread support for the concept of jihad against a foreign occupier, means that the de-radicalisation programme is likely to have limited success in discouraging young men from travelling abroad, and instead is more likely to function as an aid to reintegration into society for those who do travel abroad and then return. While there are certainly fewer cases of Saudis travelling to Iraq, this probably has more to do with the decline of al-Qaeda in Iraq's foreign recruitment and less to do with the de-radicalisation programme itself.

Progress made by Yemen in co-opting militants from 2002-05 has been cancelled out by the rise of a new generation of militants, less willing to cooperate with the government and reinforced by experienced Saudi jihadists.

In Yemen, meanwhile, the 2002-05 programme had little or no perceptible effect in reducing terrorism risks. While this was in part due to patchy implementation and a lack of resources to keep track of individuals after their release, it was also in large part due to the escape in 2006 of a number of more militant individuals who had no interest in being reconciled with the government. Among these was Nasir al-Wuhayshi, the current leader of AQAP, who forcefully argued that the terrorist campaign must be continued, and that there was no future in making concessions for the sake of detainees still being held. That year, the Yemeni al-Qaeda franchise conducted suicide bomb attacks in September on energy facilities at Marib and al-Shihr, and assassinated the chief criminal investigator in Marib. The rise of this new generation of terrorist leaders in Yemen effectively cancelled out the benefits secured by deals that the Yemeni government had made on an individual basis with a number of less radical militants. Al-Wuhayshi's group now poses the primary terrorist threat in Yemen but is also a significant factor in reducing the effectiveness of Saudi Arabia's de-radicalisation programme, since released militants can choose to abscond across the border to join AQAP.

2. Iran: Balancing the Pressures

Despite a proposal put forward by Western powers in September 2009 that would involve Iran exporting uranium abroad for further enrichment, an agreement is far from assured. Certain Western powers mistrust Iran's intentions, given the limited access it has provided the International Atomic Energy Agency (IAEA) and the likely emergence of new clandestine nuclear facilities. This means that the US and European governments will, to varying degrees, discourage new business in Iran. The US in particular is likely to push for sanctions on fuel exports while also pressuring Western companies to cease trading with Iran. Consensus exists within Iran, however, over the Islamic Republic's right to nuclear power regardless of internal opposition to Ahmadinejad's conduct of foreign policy. Dissent within the ruling elite, driven to some degree by economic interests, was exposed by Ahmadinejad's re-election. This article contains extracts from our analysis on Iran, which has focused on the commercial implications of a more comprehensive sanctions regime, as well as various war scenarios. It also addresses internal developments in Iran with the associated implications for the investment climate and foreign policy.

Context

Iran has consistently denied any intention to acquire a nuclear weapons capability and insists that its nuclear programme is intended purely for civilian purposes. Its incomplete and intermittent cooperation with the IAEA inspections and decades of hostility with the US and Israel means that Western governments base their policy towards Iran on worst-case assessments. Indeed, the UN negotiations of recent years were sparked by claims in 2002 by Iranian opposition groups that Iran was operating secret nuclear development facilities, a heavy-water production facility at Arak and an underground uranium enrichment plant at Natanz.

In September 2009, Iran revealed an additional enrichment facility at Qom, most likely under pressure following leaked information about the existence of the site to Western intelligence. Further clandestine facilities may come to light in 2010. The more complex, dispersed and well-protected the facilities are, the less likely it is that they are intended for peaceful purposes.

Nevertheless, there is no undisputed evidence that Iran intends to build nuclear weapons. The US National Intelligence Estimate (a consensus view of several US intelligence agencies) of November 2007 assessed with 'high confidence' that until the autumn of 2003, Iranian military entities were working under government direction to develop nuclear weapons. Currently, Iran operates uranium enrichment centrifuge cascades producing low-enriched uranium, contrary to the decisions of the UN Security Council. Low-enriched uranium is not suitable for military use.

Our assessment is that even now there are almost no elements of Iran's ruling establishment that have decided to gain a nuclear weapons capability as fast as possible. Our information suggests that the only decision taken so far is to make progress towards what would be needed, but to maintain strategic ambiguity. For Western policy-makers and indeed the IAEA, the difference is semantic. For Iranians, it is not.

Key Foreign Players: Strategic Considerations

Rather than a zero-sum game involving Iran on one side and the US and/or Israel on the other, the pathway and timeline for sanctions or confrontation will be determined by complex multi-player games involving the US, Russia, China, Israel and the EU-3 (the UK, France and Germany).

Members of the UN Security Council and the EU are far from unanimous about how to respond to Iran's nuclear programme. In part, this is due to Europeans, Chinese and Russians seeking to protect their commercial interests in developing Iran's oil and gas sector. Also, Iran's strategic interests in the region, including Iraq, Afghanistan, Lebanon and the Persian Gulf, make the use of force risky and give Iran a wide range of low-risk response options. At the same time, Iran's strong trade with, and cultural and religious ties to, Iraq and Dubai, would make sanctions, for example, on gasoline exports to Iran, difficult to implement.

The US

President Obama will be under pressure from the US Congress to take further unilateral sanctions on Iran, particularly if a proposal for the export of enrichment fails to come to fruition.

The US is likely to pursue multi-lateral, but not UN, sanctions targeting gasoline exports to Iran (due to limited refining capacity, Iran depends on imports for 40% of its gasoline). The US has used market regulators and its own Treasury's muscle to put pressure on European banks and other businesses to stop doing business in Iran. Companies which have been sanctioned or backed out of Iran due to US pressure include: ABN Amro, Lloyds TSB, UBS, Total, Repsol and Shell.

President Obama stated on 1 October 2009 that, 'Our patience is not unlimited. The United States will not continue to negotiate indefinitely, and we are prepared to move towards increased pressure'. However, his hands are largely tied given the present precarious positions in Iraq and Afghanistan. Obama almost certainly gets advice from the Joint Chiefs of Staff that strategic objectives in both Iraq and Afghanistan would be threatened if Iran were to become actively hostile and use proxies to apply pressure. This moderates actions and constrains policy choices, especially when the US is making a surge of effort in Afghanistan.

Russia

Russia would be likely to veto further UN sanctions on Iran.

This is despite the fact that Russian President Medvedev stated in September 2009 that in some cases sanctions were inevitable. His statement came shortly after the US said it would disband its plan for a missile-defence system in Eastern Europe. Russia, which has offered significant technical support for Iran's civil nuclear programme, will seek to maintain its extensive military and commercial ties with Iran. For Russia, this is more about money than geopolitics. In Iran, Russia has a market for its very moderate nuclear technology and weapons. The last thing Russia wants to see is a US-Iran reconciliation and a General Electric nuclear reactor at half the price and twice the quality in Iran.

China

China, which has significant energy interests in Iran, has consistently opposed the imposition of further UN sanctions against Iran.

In September 2009, China signed an oil exploration contract for the South Azadegan oilfield worth, according to official Iranian sources, $2.5 billion. This dramatically increases China's reluctance to support any significant new sanctions. Furthermore, Chinese exports of gasoline to Iran are already under way, limiting the impact of US proposals to sanction firms involved in exporting petrol to Iran. As of September 2009, China was reportedly exporting 30,000 to 40,000 bpd to Iran via third parties. For China, this is a profitable and currently legal venture that it will not wish to give up.

The EU-3

The EU-3 are probably stalling due to political pressures from their own governments to cease opening new investments in Iran, rather than obstacles being placed from the Iranian side.

The current sanctions regime approved by the UN Security Council, or the EU sanctions against Iranian banking institutions, do not specifically target the energy sector. The EU states maintain a keen interest in developing the South Pars gas field, which is estimated to hold 5.6% of the world's proven gas reserves. Companies such as Total, Repsol and ENI have not entirely pulled out from negotiations with the Iranian government over this project. However, this policy lacks coordination at the EU level and is pursued, most of the time half-heartedly, in different ways by the different governments. Italy has, for example, refrained by adopting the stance of France or Germany, at least publicly. Both France and Germany are pushing to end new investments in Iran, while not appearing keen to curtail existing ones, opened during the Khatami or early Ahmadinejad era.

Israel

Israel has repeatedly indicated that it will not let Iran acquire a nuclear weapons capability. While this does not necessarily imply that Israel will attack Iran, Israel's security doctrine has historically emphasised pre-emption.

Israel's public position is that it will take military action in order to prevent Iran from acquiring a nuclear military capability. In a February 2009 address to the Conference of Presidents of Major American Jewish Organizations, the former prime minister, Ehud Olmert, said, 'If Iran becomes nuclear there will be a major threat to the life of the State of Israel, a threat we can't tolerate, and we will not tolerate this threat and we will not allow it to happen - that I can promise you.' More recently, in May 2009, Prime Minister Netanyahu stated at the Annual AIPAC Conference, 'If I had to sum it up in one sentence, it is this: Iran must not be allowed to develop nuclear weapons.' Logistically, the Israeli Air Force (IAF) could reach most key Iranian sites. Natanz and Esfahan are at the limit for conventional air attack, with more eastern targets probably out of range without US refuelling assistance. The F15I plane has a probable maximum combat radius of 1,800 km while carrying two 2,000kg deep penetration bombs to attack the Natanz underground facility. The F16I plane's range is around 1,500 km, sufficient to attack the Arak surface facility with conventional bombs.

The IAF would have three primary flight options. The direct route from Navatim Airbase to Natanz is around 1,600 km across Iraq and would require the greatest US compliance. The most likely option, the 1,625 km northern route, would involve a 'border run' from the eastern Mediterranean through northern Syria and Iraq before heading southeast to Natanz. The Syria leg has already been successfully proven during the September 2007 attack on Syria, while the northern Iraq leg is poorly covered by US forces who could either ignore or assist. The southern route, across Jordan and again a 'border run' along Saudi-Iraqi airspace, is the longest and least likely option.

However, we assess that Israel lacks the ability to generate enough air sorties from close enough to destroy a useful amount of Iran's very well dispersed and defended nuclear programme. Iran, having learned from Israel's strike on the Iraqi nuclear plant of Osiraq in 1981, has buried, dispersed and defended its facilities. Thus Israel would have to launch a high-risk operation, with probably minimal destructive effect. It would then face the near certainty of retaliatory Iranian long-range missile strikes against Israeli population centres. However, Iranian missile stocks are limited and the Arrow ballistic defence system arguably already provides adequate defensive coverage, which the deployment of Arrow 3 in 2012-13 will further enhance.

Given the above, Israel is most likely to choose to intercept suspected military shipments and nuclear-related material heading to Iran by temporarily seizing vessels. This reportedly occurred with the Arctic Sea in August 2009, a Maltese-flagged vessel that was allegedly hijacked off Cape Verde on its way to Algeria from Finland. The Israelis claimed that it was carrying S-300 missiles to Iran from Russia (rather than timber as the Russians had said).

Probable routes for Israeli airstrikes on Iranian nuclear facilities

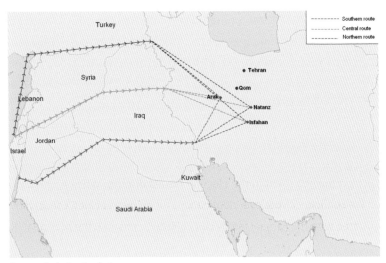

Source: Exclusive Analysis

Iran: Internal Developments

The presidential elections of 2009 exposed the degree of internal divisions within Iran's political elite. Despite the large-scale protests led by the reformists, the most effective opposition to Ahmadinejad will come from the conservatives.

Presidential elections in June 2009 resulted in a landslide victory for Ahmadinejad and the defeat of Mousavi, a former prime minister and reformist who had been expecting to win or at least force a run-off. As a result, Mousavi supporters staged a number of large protests, mainly in the capital, Tehran, which quickly began to lose momentum as state forces quelled demonstrations. The elections, however, exposed the degree of internal divisions within Iran's political elite. While conservatives and reformists equally support Iran's right to nuclear power, Ahmadinejad's opponents criticise his economic management and conduct of foreign policy.

The liberal reformists aligned with the defeated candidates Mousavi and Karroubi will probably be completely sidelined in 2010. However, a conservative opposition present in the Majles (Parliament) will probably press for incremental concessions while they ready themselves to take power at the next presidential elections, possibly through the current mayor of Tehran, Baqr Qalibaf. This conservative group, which includes Parliament Speaker Ali Larijani, remained silent in the election results dispute. While Ahmadinejad won the confidence vote over nominations for his new cabinet, conservatives associated with the Larijani family can politically constrain the president. Key episodes of Parliament-government interaction, such as the government's proposal of bills that include significant financial expenditure, or the budget law itself, will test the president's support in Parliament.

The reformist opposition to Ahmadinejad will be increasingly unable to organise protests and mobilise its supporters.

The authorities have detained and tried supporters and chief strategists of the reformist politicians and defeated presidential candidates Mousavi and Karroubi. They have jailed certain critics of the government (e.g. those who gave interviews to Persian media based outside Iran). Associates or close relatives of the top leadership are often imprisoned when the leaders publish communiqués. Such communiqués have become much less frequent, particularly from Mousavi. The country is not under formal lockdown, as the occasional disorderly protest attests, and so far the authorities have resorted to sporadic use of plain-clothes forces, rather than curfews.

The Iranian Revolutionary Guard Corps (IRGC), which has major bases around the periphery of Tehran, is unlikely to be deployed to contain protests as it would risk provoking a significant confrontation. Should this occur it would be likely to indicate a rapid escalation of unrest that could deepen hostility between contesting factions within Iran's political elites. The paramilitary wing of the IRGC (the Basij) can readily deploy well-trained and well-motivated fighters in the event of major unrest. More commonly, however, the Iranian authorities would deploy security personnel in civilian clothing, controlled by the security branch of the judiciary. This occurred in response to demonstrations in June to July 2009.

The IRGC's loyalties will prove decisive in maintaining the status quo.

The IRGC still appears to be, at least on the surface, loyal to Supreme Leader Khamenei. Indeed, a nexus exists between Supreme Leader Ayatollah Khamenei, the Revolutionary Guard's top leadership, President Ahmadinejad, the conservative majority in Parliament and the heads of all state institutions (bar the ones that Ayatollah Akbar Hashemi Rafsanjani leads - the Assembly of Experts and Expediency Council). Despite personal rivalries, especially between Ahmadinejad and some conservative MPs, this faction will most likely stick together. It effectively endorsed the election results that the Interior Ministry produced and has resolutely quashed any claim to the contrary.

The internal dynamics of this group are not entirely clear. There are signs that Khamenei is not its absolute leader and must at the very least obtain clearance from the IRGC's senior leadership before making key decisions. However, there is consensus to keep Khamenei as leader, at least in nominal form. Khamenei probably still holds the power to decide the fate of the reformist leadership. While many IRGC leaders probably favoured jailing Mousavi and Karroubi, Khamenei ultimately intervened to keep them out of jail.

If this group can retain power, the IRGC will probably monopolise foreign trade and become the sole port of call for foreign investors. However, it is likely to do this through a large network of subsidiary companies in Iran and key trade hubs such as Dubai, in order to elude probable international sanctions against its leadership.

To resist marginalisation, Rafsanjani will probably position himself as the only player able to heal internal rifts after Ahmadinejad's re-election.

Ayatollah Akbar Hashemi Rafsanjani who heads the Assembly of Experts, an 86-member body that chooses the supreme leader, is one of Iran's most influential politicians and businessmen. He was a close associate of Supreme Leader Khamenei and served as president from 1989 to 1997. Through his connections and patronage networks he can mobilise widespread support among the political and business elite. Rafsanjani is playing a complex political game in which he is trying to position himself as the 'gatekeeper' between the reformist opposition and Ahamdinejad's backers, and present himself as essential to preventing an intra-elite split from widening.

Whether Rafsanjani still possesses the influence to counter-balance the IRGC's economic and political influence is debatable, however. Rafsanjani was prevented from leading prayers on Qods day (which falls on the last day of Ramadan) in September 2009 for the first time in a quarter of a century. However, in a speech that followed, Supreme Leader Khamenei offered conciliatory words to the Hashemi family. He noted how individuals could not be convicted on the basis of third-party court testimonies, a reference to the accusations that prosecutors directed at Rafsanjani's children during the mass trials of the reformist activists following post-election unrest. Rafsanjani is probably trying to engineer a compromise between the opposing sides that would lead to the release of the dozens of high-profile reformists imprisoned in 2009.

In October 2009, reports on the alleged death of Iran's supreme leader, Ayatollah Ali Khamenei, appeared on weblogs and as well as Saudi news sites. While there was little to substantiate the reports, which may have been politically motivated, it nevertheless raises the question of succession.

In the event of Khamenei's death, the 86-member Assembly of Experts, headed by Ayatollah Rafsanjani, is charged with selecting a new supreme leader. In the interim, however, an emergency council consisting of the president, the head of the judiciary and an Islamic scholar from the Guardian Council would take over the supreme leader's duties. This council's decisions must be approved by three quarters of the Rafsanjani-led Expediency Council. Given the lack of unity within the political elite, there is likely to be some delay in the selection of the next supreme leader (which was unlike the conditions with Khamenei was selected as a successor Ayatollah Khomeini so swiftly in 1989), creating a political vacuum that the Revolutionary Guard is likely to step in to fill. We assess that the influence of President Ahmedinejad, with whom the IRGC is aligned, will also likely grow. Khamenei, who has been supreme leader for 20 years, has been uniquely able to oversee checks and balances on the influence of all of Iran's key players.

Turning Insight Into Foresight